FROM A LIMINAL PLACE

FROM A
LIMINAL
PLACE

AN ASIAN AMERICAN THEOLOGY

SANG HYUN LEE

Fortress Press

Minneapolis

Dedicated to my family:

Inn Sook
Mi Hyong, Cy, Sandra,
Jacob, and Jordan

FROM A LIMINAL PLACE
An Asian American Theology

Cover image: *Handwritten Morning Sunscape* by Delbert Michael (c. 1979)
Cover design: Laurie Ingram
Book design: PerfecType, Nashville, TN
Author photo: Kim Schmidt, Princeton Theological Seminary

Library of Congress Cataloging-in-Publication Data
Lee, Sang Hyun, 1938-
  From a liminal place : an Asian American theology / Sang Hyun Lee.
    p. cm.
  Includes bibliographical references and index.
  ISBN 978-0-8006-9668-9 (alk. paper)
  1. Asian Americans—Religious life. 2. Marginality, Social—Religious aspects—Christianity. I. Title.
  BR563.A82L44 2010
  230.089'95—dc22
                        2010013006

Manufactured in the U.S.A.

14 13 12 11 10 1 2 3 4 5 6 7 8 9 10

CONTENTS

Preface   ix

Acknowledgments   xv

Chapter 1. The Context of Asian American Theology   1

Two Dimensions of the Asian American Experience   1

Liminality and Its Creative Possibilities   5

The Marginalization of Asian Americans   11

The Dual Liminality and Marginalization of Asian
    American Women   22

The Strangers from a Different Shore   28

Liminality in the Condition of Marginalization   31

**Chapter 2. God's Strategic Alliance with the Liminal
and Marginalized**   35

Galilee as the Place of Jesus' Ministry and Galileans as
    His First Followers   38

The Liminality of Galilee and Galileans   43

The Marginalization of Galilee and Galileans   47

Chapter 3. God and Liminality   **51**

God's End in Creation   52

Liminality in God   54

The Incarnation and Liminality   59

Chapter 4. The Way of the Liminal Jesus as the Christ   **63**

Leaving Home: Jesus' Appropriation of Liminality   63

Jesus' Exercise of the Creative Potentials of His Liminality   68

The Death of Jesus Christ   79

The Resurrection of the Crucified Jesus   83

The Exaltation of Jesus Christ   86

Chapter 5. Redemption in Asian American Context   **89**

The Meaning of Atonement   89

Believers' Response to and Participation in Atonement   97

Justification of the Marginalized   101

Repentance   104

Chapter 6. Asian American Identity and the Christian Faith   **109**

Asian American Identity in a Postmodern and
     Postcolonial Context   109

Working on Asian American Identity   112

Faith and Identity   117

Identity and Narrative   119

Chapter 7. Asian American Church   **123**

Church as *Communitas* and Structure   124

Asian American Church as Refuge and Liminal Space   127

The Prophetic Ministry of Asian American Churches   132

Women and the Asian American Church   138

Marks of the Church   141

Chapter 8. The New Liminality and Asian American Discipleship 147

Openness to the New 149

Communitas with Others 151

Resistance and the "Happiness That Forgets Nothing" 154

Chapter 9. Liminality and Reconciliation 161

The Task of Reconciliation 161

The Role of Liminality in Reconciliation 164

Chapter 10. A New Heaven and a New Earth 173

Conclusion 179

Notes 183

Index 197

PREFACE

When I was young, I used to think that one did theology in order to solve some difficult theoretical problem. I do theology in this book, however, not to deal with some theoretical issue but, rather, to find some meaning to my and my fellow Asian Americans' lives in the United States. Is there any meaning or purpose in living one's entire life caught up between two worlds, belonging somewhat to both but, at the same time, not belonging wholly to either—Asia or America? What theological meaning does a life have that is spent entirely at the periphery and not at the center of a society and culture?

In this book, I propose one possible Christian theological perspective on the above questions. In order to develop such a perspective, I must search the Scriptures. But everyone reads the Scriptures from a particular context whether he or she acknowledges it or not, and the context may affect his or her reading. So I begin this book by analyzing in chapter 1 the context from which I search the Scriptures and do theology.

The Asian American experience has often been characterized as "marginality." Marginality that is the result of marginalization is also said to have two aspects: the negative aspect of being excluded by the dominant group, and the positive aspect of being a potentially creative condition. For the purpose for clarity, I use the term *marginality* for the negative situation of being excluded, and refer to the potentially creative aspect of marginality with a different term, *liminality*. Liminality is the situation of being in between two or more worlds, and includes the meaning of being located at the periphery or edge of a society.

Liminality, according to the anthropologist Victor Turner, is a transitional time in which persons are freed from social-structure hierarchy and role playing and, therefore, may be more open to what is new, experience a close communion with other persons (*communitas*), and become capable of prophetic critique of the existing social order. The creative potentials of Asian Americans' liminality, I argue, are in a frustrated and suppressed state because of the demoralizing and dehumanizing effects of marginalization.

When one approaches the biblical text from the perspective of a particular contextual background, certain matters stand out in ways that someone else with a different contextual background might not notice. Reading the Gospels with marginality and liminality in mind, I particularly noticed the fact that Jesus was a Jewish Galilean and that he conducted his public ministry primarily among Galileans. Then I also learned from historical studies that Galileans were very much a liminal and marginalized people.

Jesus' Galilean identity leads us to other theological affirmations:

1. God became incarnate as a Galilean.
2. Jesus' initial approach to Galileans in his ministry would seem to imply that it was strategic for God to do so because of Galileans' liminality and their openness to what is new. Galileans were a people with sin just as any other people. But their social location of liminality made it likely that at least some of them would be open to the radically new message of Jesus (chap. 2).
3. If God in Jesus Christ assumed a liminal situation in time and history, and if what God does in history is not capricious but rooted in God's own being, then we must posit liminality in

God. Indeed, we can see the Father's and the Son's experience
of liminality in their mutual giving of themselves to the other.
Jesus' assumption of a liminal situation in time is a repetition or
reiteration of the Father's and Son's liminal experience within
the Trinity (chap. 3). In this chapter I also outline the overall
theological framework of the theology of the colonial American
theologian Jonathan Edwards, which I believe can be the theological backbone of an Asian American theology.

Jesus was unlike other Galileans in that he was the incarnate Son
of God, the second person of the Trinity. Unlike other Galileans, Jesus,
in spite of the demoralizing effects of his marginalization, was able to
exercise all of the three creative potentials of his liminality (openness
to the new, *communitas*, prophetic knowledge and action) for the realization and personal embodiment of the reign of God. Chapter 4 traces
the ways Jesus utilized his liminality to be open to God the Father, to
build a new community, and to resist prophetically against the marginalizing forces of his day. As the new human being or a second Adam,
Jesus embodied the way Asian Americans, and all other human beings,
should live in their own liminal situation.

Chapter 5 concentrates on the climax of Jesus' public ministry,
the crucifixion, the resurrection, and the ascension. Jesus' expression
of the radical love of God that knows no boundaries, and his critique
of the oppressive policies of the political and religious authorities led
him to his death on the cross. As Jesus was dying on the cross, feeling
abandoned even by his heavenly Father, he entered an infinite space
of liminality out of which the infinite forgiving grace of God emerged
in the form of the redeeming *communitas*. Those believers who with
their own liminality join Jesus in this infinite liminality can experience
the transforming *communitas* with God and enter into an everlasting
communion with that God and a new life on earth.

Asian Americans' experience of the redeeming *communitas* with
God in Jesus is an experience of being accepted as God's children in

spite of their sinfulness, and also an experience of belonging to God's family as equal members of that family with everyone else. The resurrection of the crucified Jesus confirms the truth and reality of God's forgiving and accepting love.

Chapter 6 discusses the relationship between the Asian American Christians' faith in the God of redeeming love and their identity as Asian Americans. Identity is thought of in a nonessentialist fashion as what happens through speech, action, and relationships. An Asian American identity, therefore, is constantly constructed and dissolved and then reconstructed. Identity emerges in a liminal space. Christian faith's primary function in this identity construction is to enable Asian Americans to face up to the task of constructing their identity in the bewildering space of liminality. The unity and *telos* or goal of identity are provided by an individual's story or narrative of his or her life. In the case of a Christian, the individual's narrative is a personal appropriation of the narrative of God, or the story of the end for which God created the world.

Chapter 7 explores what Asian American churches should be in light of all that has been said up to this point. The church is a liminal space where Asian Americans can feel "safe" to be explicitly conscious of their liminal situation. The church should provide an appropriate liminal time so that the members can enter into the infinite liminality of Jesus on the cross and experience again the redeeming *communitas* with God. This chapter also outlines how the three creative potentials of liminality can be exercised by the Asian American church community for the proclamation of God's reign in today's society. The chapter ends with a reinterpretation of the Nicene Creed's four "notes" of the church from an Asian American theology's point of view.

Chapter 8 discusses some of the aspects of the Christian "style" of life for Asian Americans. Again, I present the idea of the three creative potentials of liminality appropriated in conceptualizing the nature of Christian discipleship from Asian American theology's point of view.

Chapter 9 suggests that liminality may have a crucial role to play in fulfilling the Christian responsibility of racial reconciliation.

Chapter 10 outlines briefly what the fulfilled state of God's creation would be like. This discussion could be placed at any point in a systematic theology, although here it is placed at the end. The New Heaven and the New Earth do not end history as such because the process of God's repeating of God's internal being in time and history must go on for an everlasting time.

The upshot of all this is that all Christian churches that aspire to be the churches of Jesus Christ the Galilean must situate themselves at the periphery, not at the center, of their society. Since Asian Americans are already at the periphery and in-between, it is their churches' special and particular vocation to be in-between and at the periphery. Peripherality in the sense of liminality should not lead to sectarianism, because liminality is always in a dialectical relationship with structure and, therefore, with society. Liminality's energies are inherently directed to being incorporated into society and toward an enhancement of that society.

The challenge that the perspective outlined in this book poses to the leadership in the Asian American churches is a weighty responsibility indeed. Many Asian Americans, including Christians, live the materialistically interpreted American dream as the story that governs their lives. An awareness of their liminal condition usually remains submerged under their obsessive drive for success in achieving that dream. Can the leaders of Asian American churches present their people a vision greater than that dream and convert them to love the end for which God created the world? How can church leaders arouse in their people the painful but liberating awareness of their liminality in American society? Can Asian American Christians follow the example of Christ in exercising the creative powers of their liminal situation and thereby achieve happiness in knowing the authentic meaningfulness of their existence as strangers in American society?

ACKNOWLEDGMENTS

It is my pleasure to acknowledge my indebtedness to those persons who gave me help and encouragement in writing this book. I am deeply grateful to Don Schweitzer, my former student and now a professor of theology at St. Andrews College, Saskatoon, Saskatchewan, who willingly has been my conversation partner almost every step of the way in the long process of thinking through the major portions of this book. Mark Lewis Taylor, my colleague in the department of theology at Princeton, never stopped encouraging me to develop the basic thesis of this book. I want to thank Richard Horsley of the University of Massachusetts Boston for many phone conversations about Galilee. Any errors I make about Galilee are mine, however, and not his. Others who gave me encouragement and help include Won Moo Hurh, Roy Sano, Fumitaka Matsuoka, Richard R. Niebuhr, Andrew Sung Park, Wonhee Anne Joh, Dan Migliore, Peter Paris and Rick Osmer, Kevin Park, Adam Eitel, Joseph Kim, and many others. I must mention with gratitude my most recent class on Asian American theology during the fall semester of 2009 (Clayton Chan, Kendrick Jahng, John Kim, Paul Kim, K. C. Kye, Jooho Lee, Nathan Hiroshi Mochizuki, HyeJin Shim, and Wonjae Yu). I benefited from their careful reading of the manuscript and spirited discussion. I owe a special debt to Jooho Lee, who raised several important questions of clarification and helped improve the text.

I am also grateful to Austin Presbyterian Theological Seminary and Fuller Theological Seminary for inviting me to give the Settles Lectures (1991) and the Peyton Lectures (1993), respectively. These lectures gave me an opportunity to try out my earlier formulations of some of the themes developed in this book.

I have been fortunate to have as my editors Michael West and Susan Johnson at Fortress Press. I very much appreciated Michael West's empathetic reading of what Asian American theologies are trying to say. Finally, I thank my wife, Inn Sook, for her never-failing encouragement and companionship both in this project and in life.

Chapter 1
THE CONTEXT OF ASIAN
AMERICAN THEOLOGY

TWO DIMENSIONS
OF THE ASIAN AMERICAN EXPERIENCE

There was no particular problem with my life in the United States when I thought of myself as a foreign student from Korea. All I had to do was study hard and get good grades. But when I began teaching in a small town in the Midwest with the prospect of living my entire life there, something disturbing began to emerge in my consciousness. However long I stayed in this country, I seemed to remain a stranger, an alien. People kept asking me, "Where are you from?" After fifty-three years in this country, they still ask me, "Where are you from?" And "Princeton, New Jersey" is hardly ever the correct answer to those who ask the question. Several times each and every day, someone reminds me that I do not belong here.

In the late 1960s I heard a Korean American sociologist present a paper at a conference on the Korean immigrant experience in the United States. He said that "marginality" is the term and concept that sociologists use to describe the social predicament especially of nonwhite minority peoples in this country. "I am a 'marginal' person," I said to myself. I felt rather discouraged by the word but at the same time experienced a strange kind of exhilaration from finding out a definite name for my situation in American society.

From the first time I learned of the concept of "marginality," however, I felt this concept, like my own experience of being a "stranger," ambiguously combined two elements of nonwhite people's experience in this country, one at least potentially positive, the other negative. In the preface I described the positive element of marginality as being a potentially creative condition and the negative element as being excluded by the dominant group. Everett V. Stonequist, who further developed sociologist Robert E. Park's idea of "the marginal man [*sic*]," explains these two elements in more detail. A marginal person, according to Stonequist, "is poised in psychological uncertainty *between two (or more) social worlds*; reflecting in his soul the discords and harmonies, repulsions and attractions of these worlds, one of which is often *'dominant' over the other.*"[1] Such a person "emulates and strives to be accepted by a group of which he is not yet, or *is only peripherally a member.*"[2] Stonequist states that marginality thus refers to the space "between two (or more) social worlds," and the world in which a person is marginalized is "dominant" over that person's original world.

Stonequist also noted the inherent creativity of a marginal situation as follows:

> The marginal man [*sic*] is the key-personality in the contacts of cultures. It is in his mind that the cultures come together, conflict, and eventually work out some kind of mutual adjustment and interpenetration. He is the crucible of cultural fusion. . . . Thus the practical efforts of the marginal person to solve his own problem lead him consciously or unconsciously to change the situation itself. His interest may shift from himself to the objective social conditions and launch him upon the career of a nationalist, conciliator, interpreter, reformer, or teacher.[3]

H. F. Dickie-Clark, who has paid particular attention to the role of dominant groups in causing the marginalization of minority groups, clearly analyzes the negative nature of such exclusion. According to Dickie-Clark, marginality results from a hierarchical relationship of groups in which "a resistance is offered by members of the non-marginal and dominant group, to his [the marginal person's] entry into the group and the enjoyment of its privileges." Moreover, a "barrier [is] set up by that group, that an individual in a marginal situation who possesses characteristics (those gained through acculturation) which would 'ordinarily' give him [sic] a higher status, is not granted that status." What makes a situation marginal, in other words, "lies in inconsistencies between rankings." And such inconsistencies brought about by a higher and more powerful group deny "the enjoyment by an inferior one, of their powers, privileges and opportunities."[4] In this way, Dickie-Clark's discussion helps to bring out clearly the fact that marginality is a condition affected by both status and power issues. The minority groups do not simply find themselves at the edges of their society; they are marginalized to be there.

Marginality is a spatial metaphor. To this metaphor must be added the power dynamic of the dominant group's act of marginalizing certain groups of people if one is to have an adequate picture of the predicament of Asian Americans as a people at the margins. Like other nonwhite minority groups in America, Asian Americans are not just in an "in-between" or peripheral predicament but are pushed to be there and forced to remain there by dominant power structures.

Vietnamese American theologian Peter C. Phan describes the spatial, political, and cultural dimensions of the negative aspects of being in-between as follows:

> To be betwixt and between is to be neither here nor there, to be neither this thing nor that. Spatially, it is to dwell at the periphery or at the boundaries. Politically, it means not residing at the centers of power of the two intersecting worlds

but occupying the precarious and narrow margins where the two dominant groups meet and clash, and [being] denied the opportunity to wield powers in matters of a minority, a member of a marginal(ized) group. Culturally, it means not fully integrated into and accepted by either cultural system, being *mestizo*, a person of mixed race.

Lifting up the positive dimension of Asian Americans' predicament, Phan further writes:

Being neither this nor that allows one to be both this and that. Belonging to both worlds and cultures, marginal(ized) persons have the opportunity to fuse them together and, out of their respective resources, fashion a new, different world, so that persons at the margins stand not only between these worlds and cultures but also *beyond* them. Thus being betwixt and between can bring about personal and social transformation and enrichment.[5]

Besides Phan, a significant number of Asian American scholars and writers have described the Asian Americans' situation in the United States as one of "in-between-ness" or being at the "margin" or periphery and also of being pushed or marginalized into the space of margin or periphery.[6]

As noted above, I use in this book two different terms to refer to these two elements in marginality. Marginality as the result of *marginalization* is the powerless and demoralizing space into which Asian Americans are pushed into by racism in American society. I shall use anthropologist Victor Turner's term *liminality* (*limen* the Latin word for "threshold") to refer to the positive, creative nature of the in-betweenness in marginality.

A person can enter into a liminal or in-between space without being marginalized, while marginalization (being pushed into the periphery) inevitably places a person in a liminal, peripheral, and in-between place. Liminality does not have to be marginality. But marginality includes a liminal aspect. When persons, like Asian Americans, are pushed to the liminal and peripheral places by two worlds (Asia and America), their liminality means their being in the space between two worlds and at the same time at the peripheries, edges, or margins of both worlds. Asian Americans find themselves not fully accepted by, or fully belonging to, either the American world or the Asian. White Americans who are marginalized to the periphery of American society are at the edge or margin of that society only, but not between two worlds.

By making a distinction between liminality and marginalization, we avoid the danger of romanticizing marginality. Marginalization is dehumanizing and oppressive. And the space of marginality as the space into which a minority group is marginalized is a space of dehumanization, and there is nothing good in it. The liminal space that also results from marginalization, however, has the potential of being used as a creative space of resistance and solidarity. Marginalizing space and liminal space overlap. bell hooks, an African American womanist theorist, explains, "I make a definite distinction between that marginality which is imposed by oppressive structures and that marginality one chooses as the site of resistance—as location of radical openness and possibility."[7] I choose to call hooks's second marginality "liminality."

LIMINALITY AND
ITS CREATIVE POSSIBILITIES

Victor Turner developed Arnold van Gennep's theory of the rites of passage into a general theory of social change. Like the rites of passage, according to Turner, social change involves three stages: (1) the first stage of *separation* (the departure from social structure, especially social status and social role); (2) the middle stage of *liminality* in which a person is neither one thing nor another but betwixt and between; and (3) the final state of *reaggregation* or *reincorporation* into structure with a new identity or with a new perspective on the existing structure.[8]

For Turner, liminality is a space where a person is freed up from the usual ways of thinking and acting and is therefore open to radically new ideas. Freed from structure, persons in liminality are also available to a genuine communion (*communitas*) with others. Liminal space is also where a person can become acutely aware of the problems of the existing structure. A person in a liminal space, therefore, often reenters social structure with alternative ideas of human relatedness and also with a desire to reform the existing social structure.

According to Turner, human beings cannot exist in liminality for an indefinite period. They have to enter some structure, at least for survival as human beings. Thus, social change involves a dialectic movement between liminality/*communitas* and structure. Without occasional immersion into liminality/*communitas*, society becomes static.[9]

In terms of the three phases of rites of passage, Asian Americans, or their parents or grandparents, left their original homeland and have been in the liminal or in-between phase, but have not been able to be "reincorporated" into the American structure. Cultural assimilation (being able to live and work) in this country is possible. But for Asian Americans, like other nonwhite minority groups, social or structural assimilation (becoming "one of us" with the members of the dominant group) does not occur.[10] So Asian Americans are still in the wilderness of in-between "limbo," not being able to be reincorporated fully into a social structure.[11] To a limited degree, Asian Americans do enter American structure. They use the roads, shop at the supermarket, and conduct businesses. But their life in American structure involves only what sociologists call "secondary relationships," not "primary relationships," with the dominant white population.[12] There is still no meaningful social integration.

Asian Americans have only one foot in the heart of America. At best we are still dangling at the doorstep of their newly adopted country. Many Asian American individuals have important positions deep in the American structure, but only occupationally and not sociopolitically.

They, like other Asian Americans, are still in the wilderness of liminal in-betweenness, making regular visits to their workplaces, but without enjoying genuine human contact.

Those Asian Americans who were born in the United States have only this country as their home. But at some point in their early youth, they discover that white Americans do not consider them as "one of us." They find themselves "strangers" in their own homeland. They find themselves socially located at the periphery of American society and also in the liminal space of betweenness—between their birth place, America, and the their place of "origin," Asia. They are liminal or "out of structure," both in the sense of not fully belonging to America and also in the sense of not belonging to their ancestral place back in Asia. They are at the edge of America, and also between America and Asia. They are liminal in more ways than one.

What, according to Victor Turner, are the creative potentialities of the liminal space? Turner does not make a list of these creative potentialities of liminality, but we can find the following three elements in his discussions of liminality:[13]

1. *Openness to the new.* The revitalization of a society, according to Turner, involves a dialectical movement between structure and antistructure. The antistructure is experienced as a transitional condition wherein certain individuals have left behind them the social structures (such as social roles, statutes, etc.) and entered a condition from which they can return to revitalize said structures. The condition of being freed from social structure, according to Turner, is the liminal situation of being in a "temporary antinomic liberation from behavioral norms and cognitive rules." It is a kind of social limbo or the predicament of not being at a fixed place but, rather, "betwixt and between."[14] And, for Turner, it is in this liminal experience that something new in a society can emerge. Liminality is the realm of possibility where the factors of culture may be put into "free

and 'ludic' recombination in any and every possible pattern."[15] The old social category no longer holds, and the new one is not yet applicable. Being neither "this" nor "that," those in a liminal condition are not obligated to perform the usual social duties expected of occupants of a particular status or social identity. Liminality is society's "subjunctive mood, where suppositions, desires and hypotheses, possibilities and so forth, all become legitimate."[16]

Liminality is an openness and potentiality for what is new and different. According to Turner, liminality creates a framework within which participants can experiment with the familiar elements of normative social life, reconfiguring them in novel ways and discovering new arrangements and possibilities. Persons in a liminal situation are "neither here nor there; they are betwixt and between the positions assigned and arrayed by law, custom, convention and ceremonial."[17]

Theorists of change process also talk about the discomforting but necessary and creative stages in any transitional process. All changes have a departure, an in-between place of neutrality, and a reaggregation or new beginning. The neutral period of transition from the old to the new is a frightening period because the guidance and validation by the old situation have been left behind and the future is yet indeterminate. It is a chaotic period. But as William Bridges points outs, this "chaos is not a mess, but rather is the primal state of pure energy to which the person returns for every true new beginning."[18]

2. *The emergence of* communitas. According to Turner, liminality is not only an openness for society's new possibilities but is also conducive to genuine human community. Turner uses the Latin term *communitas* to distinguish the spontaneous, egalitarian, and direct modality of human relationship from "an area of common living."[19] It is when individuals have set aside social roles and status that they can experience a mode of

relationship in which people "confront one another not as role players but as 'human totals,' integral beings who recognizably share the same humanity."[20] *Communitas* is "a generic bond underlying or transcending all particular cultural definitions and normative ordering of social ties."[21] *Communitas* is "men [*sic*] in their wholeness wholly attending."[22] Such a genuine human communion, in other words, cannot be programmed or manufactured through structure, but spontaneously emerges precisely when programs and structure are left behind and when individuals are freed to relate to one another completely on an egalitarian ground. So for Turner, "communitas breaks in through the interstices of structure, in liminality; and at the edges of structure, in marginality; and from beneath structure, in inferiority."[23]

Communitas, according to Turner, cannot stand alone, however. "The immediacy of communitas gives way to the mediacy of structure" because structure is necessary "if the material and organizational needs of human beings are to be adequately met."[24] But at the same time, structure without egalitarian values of *communitas* becomes inhospitable to human beings. Turner assumes here that *communitas* as a communion of human beings as equals is an essential human need, an "indispensable human social requirement."[25] For a society to function properly, according to Turner, the experience of *communitas* must infuse structure with antistructural values and in so doing transform everyday social structures.[26]

3. *The creative space for prophetic knowledge and action.* Liminality is conducive to an openness to the new and also to *communitas*. Now we turn to what liminality is capable of vis-à-vis the structure and the center. To be in between and at the edge is to attain a distance from structure and the center. In liminality, there is not only a kind of freedom to be, think, and act in a way not quite "allowed" in the structure or the center but also

a freedom to be critical of the structure and the center both negatively and constructively. Liminality is the creative space where one has the freedom to break down the status quo and also the freedom to rebuild it in a different way.

On the "negative" side, liminality is the space where a critical knowledge of the existing structure is possible. For Turner, the openness for the new that is possible in liminality is inherently an openness to a knowledge of what is problematic with the status quo—that is, an openness to be critical of the way things are in the structure and at the center. Liminality is a space where persons can "'play' with the elements of the familiar and defamiliarize them." "Novelty emerges from unprecedented combinations of familiar elements."[27] Thus, "liminality . . . raises basic problems for social structural man [sic]" because it "invites him [sic] to speculation and criticism."[28] In short, from the point of view of social structure, liminality is "essentially ambiguous, unsettled . . . unsettling," and consequently, "subversive."[29] As Bobby Alexander paraphrases Turner, liminality's "'subjunctivity' or 'potentiality' stands in conflict with social structure, then, since the alternatives it offers stand opposed to structure, which consists of social boundaries."[30]

It is important to stress that for Turner liminality not only provides the capacity to be critical and subversive about what is wrong with the structure and the center but also generates a "positive" and transformative capacity. The antistructure of liminality generates new ideas and new models for society.[31] Turner writes:

> These liminal areas of time and space—rituals, carnivals, dramas, and latterly films—are open to the play of thought, feeling, and will; in them are generated new models, often fantastic, some of which may have sufficient power and plausibility to replace eventually the force-backed political and jural models that control the centers of a society's ongoing life.[32]

In sum, liminality's creative potential consists in its capacity (1) to be open to what is new, (2) to generate *communitas* as the alternative human relatedness, and (3) to challenge and transform the existing society by prophetic and subversive knowledge and criticism, envisioning and enacting new ideas and models.

As I noted earlier, the creativity of liminality does not exist in its pure form in the case of Asian Americans. Asian Americans' liminality exists within the condition of marginalization. Their liminal creativity is therefore suppressed, frustrated, and distorted. Under the condition of dehumanizing marginalization, Asian Americans' liminal creativity cannot be exercised. It may also be expressed in distorted ways. Asian Americans' excessive zeal to send their children to prestigious universities and colleges and their self-sacrificing pursuit after the materialistically interpreted "American Dream" may be examples of the distorted expressions of the creative energies inherent in their liminality. Marginalization therefore deprives Asian Americans of their particular vocation of exercising their liminal creativity for the betterment of American society.

How can Asian Americans attain the moral and spiritual power to withstand the destructive consequences of marginalization and become able to exercise their liminal creativity in authentic ways? What values should guide the exercise of their liminal creativity? I present a Christian theological outlook in this book that is intended to respond to these and other related questions.

Having discussed the liminal nature of the Asian American experience, I next turn to the Asian American experience of being marginalized.

THE MARGINALIZATION OF ASIAN AMERICANS

People are dehumanized and oppressed in many different ways, and the determinative factors vary: for example, race, ethnicity, culture, gender, age, education, economic class, job, and so forth. White American people with low income would be dehumanized economically with consequences in some other areas of their lives. White American women are dehumanized by sexism. But neither low-income white Americans nor white American women are alienated on the basis of their skin color, their race. For Asian Americans, race appears to be the all-important factor for their marginalization. However, the general impression in the mind of the American public at large and even in the minds of many Asian Americans is that white racism against Asian Americans does not exist. Especially after the Civil Rights Act of 1964, many believe racism is a thing of the past or at least on the wane.

Anecdotal reports and scholarly studies, however, indicate that Asian Americans experience serious racist discrimination. Racism against Asian Americans is individual, institutional, and cultural. Racism is bigger than individuals. When I meet and converse with a white individual in a one-to-one situation, I usually have a fine time and I usually do not find the wall of racism blocking our interaction. But as soon as another white person who is known both to me and my white conversation partner enters our discourse, the white persons will start talking to each other as if totally oblivious to my presence. Every time this happens, white individuals appear to be under the demands of some power greater than they. Racism is a part of the American culture in which white individuals live. When two or more white individuals are together, the racist culture takes over, and white individuals ineluctably and thoughtlessly act according to the cues from that culture.

Racism is bigger than white individuals also in that racism is institutional and systematic. Racial profiling by police is a well-known fact. Institutions of higher learning recruit minority students with the presumed aim of making their campuses more diverse and inclusive. But the curricula of those schools never include an adequate number of courses that are designed to meet the needs of racial ethnic minority

students. Many institutions of higher learning also adopt and adver-
tise "diversity" as their goal in faculty hiring. However, unless their
image of "excellence" as a "Euro-American scholar well recognized by
other Euro-American scholars and their guilds" is modified, the goal of
diversity will end up only as a slogan and window dressing.

Institutional racism in the American justice system is well known.
The Leadership Conference on Civil Rights, a Washington, D.C.-based
civil rights coalition, issued a report in 2000 entitled "Justice on Trial:
Racial Disparities in the American Criminal Justice System." Among
the statistics included in the report is the fact that blacks who kill whites
are sentenced to death twenty-two times more frequently than blacks
who kill blacks and seven times more frequently than whites who kill
blacks. The report also notes that a black youth is six times more likely
to be locked up than a white youth, even when charged with a similar
crime and when neither has a prior record.[33]

But individual acts of discrimination, though isolated and subtle,
are not to be ignored. Scholars studying anti-Asian American racism
recently have begun to pay particular attention to the isolated and subtle individual acts of discrimination against Asian Americans as having a most serious impact upon the psychological and physical health
of the victims. The first large-scale study of the effects of racism on
Asian Americans, entitled "A Nationwide Study of Discrimination and
Chronic Health Conditions Among Asian Americans," appeared in the
July 2007 issue of *American Journal of Public Health*. This study of a
nationally representative sample of Asian Americans found that "the
accumulation of tolls related to discrimination on an everyday basis
may contribute to allostatic load (the 'wear and tear' of body systems
resulting from an accumulation of stressors over time), erode protective
resources such as wealth and social support, and lead to chronic health
conditions."[34] More specifically, prolonged exposure to discrimination
is a contributing factor to heart disease, pain, respiratory illnesses, and
other chronic health conditions.

The Reasons for the Invisibility
of Anti-Asian American Racism

The impact of the subtle individual acts of discrimination upon Asian Americans has much to do with the reasons why anti-Asian American racism has thus far been so difficult to talk about. One reason has to do with the myth of Asian Americans as the so-called model minority. This myth, disseminated widely by the mass media, holds that the economic and educational successes of many Asian immigrants prove that they are not really discriminated against and that America is still a land of opportunity. The "model minority" idea has many problems. It draws people's attention to those Asian American young people who have gone to Ivy League schools and to the success of some Asian immigrant small-business establishments. What it ignores, however, are such realities as the heavy involvement of multiple family members in these Asian immigrant small businesses (which often includes a punishing fourteen- to sixteen-hour workday), which makes their per capita income much lower than that of white laborers. The concept also ignores many Asian immigrant youth who experience severe psychological problems in coping with their deeply alienated predicament. It has been further pointed out that the concept of "model minority" only serves a racist political function. Sociologists Won Moo Hurh and Kwang Chung Kim list the following practical functions of the "model minority" idea:

> (1) exclusion of Asian Americans from social programs supported by public and private agencies (benefit-denying/fund-saving function); (2) disguise of Asian Americans' underemployment (institutional racism promoting function); (3) justification of the American open social system (system preserving function); (4) displacement of the system's fault to less-achieving minorities (victim blaming function); and (5) anti-Asian sentiment and activities (resentment reinforcing function).[35]

In short, the myth of "model minority" only serves, as Wesley Woo has pointed out, to maintain the racist status quo and "mask the real issue—that Asians, like other people of color, are victims of institutional racism."[36]

Another reason it is sometimes hard to talk about racism against Asian Americans is the present-day American situation of the white-black paradigm in the common discourse—a discourse in which the experiences of Asian Americans as a "middle minority," a buffer people between the whites and the blacks, are often trivialized and dismissed. Gary Y. Okihiro explains:

> That marginalization of Asians, in fact, within a black and white racial formation, "disciplines" both Asian Americans and Asians and constitutes the essential site of Asian American oppression. By seeing only black and white, the presence and absence of all color, whites render Asians, American Indians, and Latinos invisible, ignoring the gradations and complexities of the full spectrum between the racial poles.[37]

In this situation, you are either black or white. Asian Americans are often perceived, especially by blacks, as a people who want to be white. If Asian Americans cry racism, they are considered hypersensitive. This predicament has led Elaine H. Kim of the University of California, Berkeley, to call for the creation of a "third space"—the space where Asian Americans can have their experiences recognized for what they are without being dismissed via the white/black dichotomy.[38] In any case, it is necessary that Asian Americans assert both the validity of their own experiences as Asian Americans and their sense of solidarity with blacks and other minority groups.

The third reason for the invisibility of anti-Asian American racism sometimes stems from Asian Americans themselves. For one thing, the awareness of white racism requires that nonwhite people, at least to some degree, adopt the white American society as their reference group—that is, the group which they, at least to some degree, would like to join. For Asian Americans who do not consider white America their world (as is the case for many recent arrivals) or who for whatever reason choose to confine their lives mostly to their ethnic enclaves, white people's attitudes are typically insignificant. These Asian Americans are still objectively marginal in American society, but they would not have the subjective or personal awareness of their marginality. They may be aware of racism in this county, but it is not much of a personal problem.[39]

There are also Asian Americans who take up an extreme assimilationist perspective and try to ignore the white racism they encounter. Some may even accept racism as a price they are willing to pay for access to the American Dream. For these and possibly other reasons, anti-Asian American white racism is often dismissed as the result of hypersensitivity or even as something amusing.

Still another reason why anti-Asian American racism is not taken seriously is that incidents of anti-Asian American discrimination are usually thought of as "isolated discrimination." "Isolated discrimination" is defined as "harmful action taken intentionally by a member of a dominant group against members of a subordinate racial or ethnic group without being socially embedded in the larger organizational or community context."[40] Isolated discrimination is then distinguished from such large-scale and organized acts of discrimination as the Chinese Exclusion Act of 1882, the Asian Exclusion Act of 1924, and the internment of Japanese and Japanese American citizens in 1942. "Isolated discrimination," then, is taken to be "isolated incidents" and therefore not really significant. But are the incidents of isolated discrimination really so isolated and thus not really significant? Personally, when I have encountered such isolated incidents of discrimination, I could not dismiss them as unimportant.

Here are some samples of isolated racist incidents.

- I go to a shopping center to buy perfume for my wife for Christmas. I patiently stand at the counter and wait for one of the salespersons to become available. Then a white woman walks up to the counter. The salesperson, who knows very well how long I have been standing there, ignores me and waits on the white lady first.
- One or two white friends and I walk into a store because I need to purchase something. I ask the person at the counter if the store has the item. The salesperson will usually look to my two white friends to give the answer and never look at me.
- I walk into a flower shop. Two white men sitting on the front steps greet me, "Hey, Boy!"
- At the airport, I stand in line to check in at the "Premier Members" counter. (For some years I used to fly a lot and had a "Premier Executive" membership with one of the airlines.) A white lady in line behind me taps on my shoulder and says, "Are you sure you are in the right line? This is for Premier Members only!"

I could go on and on, but I am beginning to feel "cheap" writing down these stories. My feeling cheap, however, is a symptom of the fact that I have for so long repressed and internalized these insults, telling myself that a "big person" (a minister and a professor) like me should not make a big deal out of these little things and instead take the "high road." But those "little" incidents of insults occur sometimes more than once a day, day after day, week after week, month after month, year after year, decade after decade.

These isolated incidents are not isolated in their impact upon the victim. Writing about the isolated incidents of racism to which African Americans are subjected, sociologist Joe Feagin points out that when those acts "accumulate over months, years, and lifetimes, the impact on a black person is far more than the sum of the individual instances." They add up, in other words, in terms of the amount of humiliation and anger. History cannot be dismissed. Feagin observes: "Particular acts, even anti-locution that might seem minor to white observers, are freighted not only with one's past experience of discrimination but also with centuries of racial discrimination directed at the entire group, vicarious oppression that still includes racially translated violence and denial of access to the American Dream."[41]

The Significance of the "Subtle Discrimination" against Asian Americans

Since the civil rights movement of the 1960s, the incidents of blatant, overt, and intentional incidents of racial discrimination have certainly decreased. Studies show, however, that racism still persists in this country. According to many scholars, racism has only "evolved into more subtle, ambiguous, and unintentional manifestations." The "'old fashioned' type where racial hatred was overt, direct, and often intentional, has increasingly morphed into a contemporary form that is subtle, indirect, and often disguised."[42] The subtle discrimination is not an incidental matter. And racism affects Asian Americans primarily in this subtle form of discrimination.

This "new" manifestation of racism is called by scholars "racial microaggressions," and has been likened to carbon monoxide, "invisible, but potentially lethal."[43] They are often overlooked and unacknowledged," but prolonged subjection to them, as noted earlier, can lead to serious chronic health problems. Racial microaggressions have been defined as "brief and commonplace daily verbal, behavioral and environmental indignities, whether intentional or unintentional, that communicate hostile, derogatory or negative racial slights that potentially have harmful or unpleasant psychological impact on the target person or group."[44] Derald Wing Sue points out that "this contemporary form of racism is many times over more problematic, damaging and injurious to persons of color than overt racist acts."[45] Here are some themes that run through racist microaggressive acts.[46]

- *Theme 1: Alien in One's Own Land.* The typical examples are questions or remarks like, "Where are you from?" or "You speak English so well." The questioner or speaker might not have intended any harm at all, but what Asian Americans "hear" is that they do not belong and are not "real" Americans even though they might have been born here.

- *Theme 2: Ascription of Intelligence.* Many participants in this study describe their teachers and fellow students making statements such as "You are really good at math" and "You people always do well in school." The conscious intent of these statements might have been to compliment Asian Americans. But Asian Americans reported feeling pressured and trapped to conform to a stereotype they had nothing to do with.

- *Theme 3: Denial or Racial Reality.* Asian American participants reported some white persons saying to them, "Asians are the new whites." Statements such as this have the effect of denying Asian Americans' experiential reality of bias and discrimination.

- *Theme 4: Exoticization of Asian American Women.* One Chinese American woman participant in the study reported, "White men believe that Asian women are great girlfriends, wait hand and foot on men, and don't back-talk or give them shit and that Asian women have beautiful skin and are just sexy and have silky hair." Other Asian American women in the study reported similar experiences. Again, the white American men might have meant to praise Asian American women, but the women felt that they were "needed for the physical needs of white men and nothing more," and that they were considered only as "passive companions to white men."

- *Theme 5: Invalidation of Interethnic Differences.* Asian Americans often are asked, "Are you a Chinese?" Their new white acquaintances often make statements such as, "Oh, my ex-girlfriend was a Chinese," "My roommate in college was a Japanese," and the like. The intent of those who make such remarks might have been to indicate that they are familiar with Asians, but the message received is that all Asians are either Chinese or Japanese, and that most Asians are familiar with each other.

- *Theme 6: Pathologizing Cultural Values/Communication Styles*. In academic classes, verbal participation is usually taken to mean a higher intelligence and ability. Some Asian American students are under the traditional Asian cultural tradition that values silence, and they are penalized for their cultural values.

- *Theme 7: Second-Class Citizenship*. A typical story involves a Korean American woman participant in the study, who spoke of dining with white friends. Although she frequently orders the wine, it is usually her friends who are asked to taste and approve the wine selection. She then feels snubbed and ignored. When Asian Americans enter a white-owned restaurant, they are often taken to a table at the back of the restaurant, even when there are many more "desirable" tables available. The message is that the restaurant is not pleased to have them as customers.

- *Theme 8: Invisibility*. Many participants reported that especially when racism is discussed, they are usually ignored. One Chinese American woman who participated in the study stated that "Some times I feel like there is a lot of talk about black and white, and there is a high Asian population here and where do we fit into that?" When racism is discussed Asian Americans are often thought of as whites, as having no experience of racism, or are simply ignored.

In addition to these themes of subtle racism identified in the study of Sue and his colleagues, social activist Gloria Yamato has instructively identified other kinds of racism experienced by Asian Americans.[47]

She categorizes white racism into four types: (1) aware/ blatant racism, (2) aware/covert racism, (3) unaware/unintentional racism, and (4) unaware/self-righteous racism.

1. *Aware/Blatant Racism.* Yamato reports that she heard it said that "the aware/blatant is preferable if one must suffer," because one can try to get out of the way before getting hurt.

2. *Aware/Covert Racism.* Apartments are suddenly no longer vacant or rents suddenly go outrageously high when persons of color inquire about them. Job vacancies are suddenly filled and persons of color are fired for vague reasons.

3. *Unaware/Unintentional Racism.* When you say something to a white person with a clear voice and perfect pronunciation of the words, she or he will often respond, "What?" It is quite clear that the white person simply assumed that this nonwhite person could not speak English very well, and that with that presumption the person did not really listen or hear. When white people talk to nonwhite persons, they will often speak at a higher pitch than they normally speak, again assuming that the nonwhite person would not understand English very well.

4. *Unaware/Self-Righteous Racism.* White persons sometimes expect and demand that a Japanese be "more Japanese" than he or she is. Many years ago, my wife and I invited an acquaintance to a dinner. We wanted to give her the best dinner we could possibly prepare. So we served a beautiful piece of broiled steak with potato and everything else that goes with it. Although she seemed to enjoy every piece of the meat (including the fat along the edge), she was extremely unhappy, saying, "You should have prepared a Korean meal!" She appeared unhappy and disappointed throughout the visit. We felt she would not allow us to be "American." We felt she was thoroughly offended by our trying to be "American."

THE DUAL LIMINALITY
AND MARGINALIZATION
OF ASIAN AMERICAN WOMEN

Asian American women face a dual or double marginalization and also a dual liminality. Asian American women, just as Asian American men, experience the in-betweenness of not really belonging to either the American society in which they live or their original home in Asia that they left behind years ago. Asian American women are liminal in their social location.

The in-betweenness of Korean women's identity living in the United States is one of the themes of Teresa Hak Kyung Cha's highly creative and complex literary work, *Dictee*. Commenting on *Dictee*, literary critic Elaine Kim writes:

> *Dictee* is in many ways a contradictory text, its paradoxes rooted in Cha's location in the interstitial outlaw spaces between Korea and America, north and south, inside and outside, and between the world of Western artist and the specific Korean nationalist impulses she inherited from her mother. But although she focuses on the "in-between"—the cracks, crevices, fissures, and seams that, when revealed, challenge hypnotic illusions of seamless reality—Cha insists on the specificity of her Korean American identity. For her, the in-between is a personal dwelling place that makes survival possible, and to ignore the importance of her Korean American identity is to deny that existence and self-hood. In this open space of liminality, Cha engages in the activity of retrieving from the past songs that were once forbidden and also registers resistance to the official accounts of the past written by the dominating powers as she strives to work out an authentic though indeterminate self.[48]

Many Asian American women experience liminality of another sort—the wilderness they enter when they reject the patriarchal sexism in which they lived according to the rules and roles that men had determined. It has been reported that many Asian American women feel freed and liberated from the patriarchal family system back home when they come to the United States. This awareness that women could live a liberated life has tended to encourage some of them to reject the sexism in their family or in church life here in their newly adopted country. Women writers have described the vacuum or a world without fixed norms and rules that they face as they leave behind the male-dominated way of life. Speaking autobiographically about the process of her "becoming woman," Penelope Washburn writes:

> A young woman must reject her mother's definition of female identity in order to allow herself the possibility of formulating a sense of personal identity. Until she rejects it, she will be unable to accept those aspects of her mother and her mother's interpretation of sexuality that are part of herself and to integrate them into a new personal value system. . . . The young woman experiences ambiguity concerning leaving home, for leaving home implies loneliness, risk, and taking responsibility for oneself and one's body. Separation from the secure worldview makes one vulnerable and confused about how to make choices, what to do, what paths to follow, and which relationships to pursue.[49]

For women to come out of this personal crisis "graciously," according to Washburn, is to gain "a new faith, a new value structure, and a new sense of personal identity." The time of ambiguity and vulnerability that Washburn speaks about is a time of liminality, an experience necessary for change.

Carol Christ finds in many women writers the theme of women's spiritual quest involving an "experience of nothingness." Christ writes,

> Experiencing nothingness, women reject conventional solutions and question the meaning of their lives, thus opening themselves to the revelation of deeper sources of power and value. The experience of nothingness often precedes

an awakening, similar to a conversion experience, in which the powers of being are revealed. A woman's awakening to great powers grounds her in a new sense of self and a new orientation in the world. Through awakening to new powers, women overcome self-negation and self-hatred and refuse to be victims.[50]

Like liminality, the experience of nothingness that Christ speaks about is an experience of having left the way things have always been and of being open to radically new possibilities. Asian American women who reject the male-dominated world first enter such a world of nothingness in which the old ways of thinking dissipate and new ways of thinking have to be constructed.

Rita Nakashima Brock, speaking as an Asian American woman, prefers the term *interstices* to either liminality or marginality and describes with a great depth and breadth what she considers to be not only the Asian American women's experience but the experience of both Asian American women and men. Brock writes, "Asian Pacific Americans participate in a variety of worlds. . . . Interstitial refers to the places in between, which are real places, like the strong connective tissue between organs in the body that link the parts."[51] It is Brock's conviction that an authentic and constructive existence for Asian American women and men calls for what she calls "interstitial integrity." To be authentically Asian American, in other words, means to face with honesty and courage the reality of our interstitiality and live out the possibilities inherent in that predicament.

For Brock, interstitiality points to the Asian American experience, which not only includes a relationship to the hegemony of the dominant culture but is the whole of it. The term *interstitiality*, Brock points out, better describes "the complexities of spiritual journeys of APA [Asian Pacific American] women."[52] In her articulation of the "interstitiality" of the Asian American experience, Brock correctly points out the multifaceted, multilayered nature of that experience. The concept of liminality, as Turner develops it, is very similar to the basic character of interstitiality that Brock speaks about. Liminality does not primarily relate to the hegemony of the dominant culture but, rather, refers to the "in-betweenness," the "fluidity," and the "unfixedness" of interstitiality. To be liminal is to be out of structure. Therefore, I submit that liminality and interstitiality have to do with a similar situation. Brock's discussion of interstitiality, however, effectively points out the depth and breadth of the fluidity, complexity, and multifaceted nature of Asian Americans' liminal predicament. I shall return to Brock when I discuss Asian Americans' identity.

Thus, Asian American women's liminality is dual. They are liminal in that they are in a situation between two or more cultural and social worlds and also in that at least some of them experience liminality as they reject their previous lives under patriarchy. Asian American women's liminality is therefore more intense and more bewildering than that experienced by Asian American men. Christian educator Inn Sook Lee reports in her study of over fifty Asian American women that they are all, without exception, aware of their marginalization in American society.[53]

Thus far we have discussed only the duality or doubleness of Asian American women's liminality. It must be noted that their marginalization is also dual or triple. Asian America women, like Asian American men, are marginalized by white racism in this country. Inn Sook Lee has pointed out that constant racial teasing (e.g., being called "Chinks," "slant-eyes," etc.) to which Asian American school girls are subjected in schools can result in low self-esteem, negative body images, and eating disorders.[54] Asian American women live with the white American orientalist stereotypes of them as subservient, obedient, passive, hard working, and exotic. Sociologist and feminist scholar Esther Ngan-Ling Chow observes that "Asian American women themselves become convinced that they should behave in accordance with these stereotyped expectations." Chow adds: "But if they act accordingly, they are then criticized for doing so, becoming victims of the stereotypes imposed by others."[55]

Asian American women are intensely devoted to their families and churches even though these two institutions also marginalize and exploit them. In a land where Asian Americans are "perpetual foreigners," their families are the primary sources of comfort and encouragement, and the families' well-being or survival attains utmost importance. Asian American women are usually totally dedicated to their families, especially to the education of their children.

But the patriarchal, sexist culture still prevails in many Asian American households. The unbalanced workload Asian American women assume at work and at home is one of the indications of their subordination to men. According to studies by sociologists Kwang Chung Kim and Won Moo Hurh, over one-third of Korean immigrants in the Chicago area are owners of small, family-run businesses. The majority of the wives of Korean small-business owners work at the store in order to save on labor costs. According to Kim and Hurh's study, the owners work on average 58.1 hours a week, and their wives work 56.6 hours a week.[56] That represents a full day's work for every day of the week. On top of their work at the shop, the study reports that wives regularly take care of four out of the six primary household tasks. Husbands take care of the disposal of the garbage and the management of the family budget, while wives do the grocery shopping, housekeeping, laundry, and dishwashing. Children sometimes help their mothers, but the burden mainly falls on the wives. Kim and Hurh conclude, "This means that in addition to their full-time business involvement, most of the working wives perform the four items predominantly when they come home from work."[57]

Much of any amount of time that might be left for Korean immigrant women is spent in fulfilling their responsibilities at their ethnic churches. In Korean immigrant churches, men hold the offices and make the official decisions while women stay in the kitchen preparing meals. Women are sometimes elected to hold offices but they have a difficult time exercising their gifts of leadership.

One woman at a Korean immigrant church was appointed by the session as the chair of a committee. She tells the story, however, of how the members of the committee (all male) always met without letting her know and made all the decisions without the presence of the female chairperson. What is astounding is not only what the male committee members did but also the fact that such illegal behavior and decision making by the men were not questioned but accepted by the church as a whole. The woman chairperson eventually submitted her resignation.[58]

What makes the situation more serious is the fact that many Korean immigrant women have felt liberated from the traditional rule that women should stay at home and have developed their personal gifts through higher education in this country. They naturally look for opportunities to serve the church in leadership positions. One highly educated Korean woman worked very hard in the kitchen and elsewhere in the church as opportunities were given her with the hope that she might eventually be elected to the eldership. Eventually the church did recognize her ability and contributions. But the church did this by electing not her, but her husband, to eldership. Her husband was also a very capable person but had not really worked as hard as his wife did. Highly educated women in Korean immigrant churches therefore look for opportunities outside the church to make leadership contributions.[59]

This is not to say that all the women in Korean immigrant churches are unhappy and frustrated. Many women who accept the very privatized, spiritualized, and depoliticized piety that characterizes many Korean immigrant churches experience a deep contentment and happiness by finding great spiritual tranquility in the church's religious life and by faithfully fulfilling their self-sacrificial duties to the family and the church. Ai Ra Kim, a Korean American clergywoman and church leader, points out that some Korean immigrant women are simply so fatigued from running a business, taking care of the family (including her husband), and then working at the church that they just go along with the traditional ways of Korean culture and find absolutely no energy to question the church's dominant structures.[60]

In recent years, many English-speaking Korean American Christian congregations have emerged, often completely independent from the first-generation immigrant churches. In these highly American-acculturated congregations patriarchal sexism also prevails. Men usually hold the highest leadership positions and conduct the Bible studies. Sermons are almost always delivered by men. The second-generation women are usually highly educated. So they are keenly discouraged when they find themselves playing only subordinate roles in the church leadership. Peter Cha and Grace May, writing in a recent book, *Growing Healthy Asian American Churches*, tell the story of Christy, who after an extensive experience as a leader of a college campus ministry came back to her home church with the hope of launching a second-generation young adult ministry. To her great disappointment, the church leaders and members told her what she could and could not do as a woman. She was discouraged from leading a coed Bible study group, serving as a member of the praise team, and even teaching a Sunday school class. The only ministry opportunities that were available for her were in the nursery and the children's program. After much agonizing, Christy left her home church. Cha and May note that recent studies show that the strong ethos of gender hierarchy in the English-speaking congregations are "particularly offensive to second-generation women who are well-educated and have professional careers." "Many, like Christy," according to Cha and May, "may decide to leave their Asian congregations to find a church where they can fully exercise their gifts."[61]

THE STRANGERS
FROM A DIFFERENT SHORE

So, white racism functions as the barrier that pushes Asian Americans out of the center of American society and keeps them at the edges of that society. Other factors also marginalize Asian Americans. For some, economic or educational factors may also make them marginal. Asian American women suffer from a double marginalization because of the sexism that exists both in the white American society and also within their own Asian American communities. Without diminishing the significance of these other determinants of Asian Americans' marginalization, it is still true, I believe, to say that white racism is the most universal determinant—a factor that applies to all Asian Americans' marginalization.

The racism barrier keeps Asian Americans from achieving what sociologists call "structural assimilation." Most Asian immigrants have no problem in the area of "cultural assimilation"—the adoption of many of white America's cultural values and mores, and the attainment of sufficient linguistic and social skills to function in white American society. Those Asian Americans who are born here, of course, have all the cultural traits of their white American peers.

But "structural assimilation" is quite another matter. This kind of assimilation means Asian Americans' becoming truly "one of us" in white American society and having the same privileges and "life chances" as white people. But this does not happen to Asian Americans who, in the eyes of the dominant group, are never "one of us." Recent studies of Korean immigrants in the Chicago and Los Angeles areas show that regardless of the length of their stay in this country, their educational levels, or their professional and economic attainments, "structural assimilation" does not really happen to them, and they tend to gravitate around their ethnic enclaves.[62] Some first-generation Korean immigrants' continuing problems with English and also their inevitable human tendency to cling to the comforts of their ethnic communities may also function to prevent "structural assimilation." But the primary factor for Asian Americans' exclusion from the center of white society is the barriers set up by the white dominant group. I have heard so many stories of American-born second- or third-generation Korean American students on college and university campuses running into white students and sometimes faculty who ask them with surprise, "How come you speak English so well?" In other words, race "sticks" for us Asian Americans. Korean American sociologist Won Moo Hurh concludes:

> Non-white immigrants may attain a high degree of cultural assimilation (adoption of American life-style), but structural assimilation (equal life-chances) is virtually impossible unless the immutable independent variable, "race," becomes mutable through miscegenation or cognitive mutation of the WASP. Koreans are no exception to this *Lebensschiksal*.[63]

As the title of Ronald Takaki's landmark history of Asian Americans has it, they are indeed "strangers from a different shore." Speaking about the early Asian immigrants who came to America to make a fortune, Takaki writes: "And so they entered a new and alien world where they would become a racial minority, seen as different and inferior, and whereby they would become 'strangers.'"[64] The white racist barriers that prevent "structural assimilation" for Asian Americans are precisely the reason why the straight-line theory of assimilation does not apply to Asian immigrants. According to that theory, an immigrant would arrive in this country and go through a period of cultural adaptation which would naturally lead to social adaptation—that is, a total acceptance by the white group as "one of us." In fact, even if a white European immigrant does not totally adapt to the American style of life and maintains an attachment to his or her ethnic heritage, such an immigrant, however, would still be accepted by the white population in this country as "one of us" almost immediately. Think of an immigrant from Germany, who hardly speaks English. When that person walks down the main street in practically any town or city in this country, he or she will be seen as "an American."

But straight-line assimilation does not happen to nonwhite immigrants such as Asian immigrants. An Asian American person may speak

English very well, adopt a name like Nancy, John, or Peter, and may have even been born in this country; but when this Asian American walks down that main street, she or he is an alien, a stranger. The idea of America as a "melting pot" in practice has always been a demand by the white dominant group for a "transmuting pot"—namely, the non-white person's rejection of (or at least not asserting) his or her own cultural heritage. The message of the white dominant culture to non-white persons has always been, "Why can't you be like us?" No person can remain whole when his or her cultural persona is fundamentally disrespected. My point here simply is that for nonwhite persons in this country, cultural adaptation does not lead to social acceptance by the dominant group.

LIMINALITY IN THE CONDITION OF MARGINALIZATION

Having looked at each of the two dimensions of the particular marginality experience of Asian Americans, it is necessary to see how those two dimensions are mutually related. In short, Asian Americans' liminality exists in a particular context—namely, in the context of the exclusion by the dominant group in America. Asian Americans do not experience liminal in-betweenness as a temporary condition or as a creative opportunity; they are pushed to liminality and are coercively made to stay there by the barriers set up by the racist center. Their liminality does not naturally lead to reaggregation or entrance or reentrance into structure, as would be the case in a normal change process.

I wrote earlier about the creative potentials of the liminal condition. Such potentials would still be in Asian Americans' marginality; but those creative potentials are repressed, thwarted, and frustrated by the second aspect of their marginality experience. The dehumanizing effect of the second aspect of marginality often debilitates the first aspect of Asian Americans' liminal creativity by taking away from them the courage and self-respect needed to face up to the creative challenge of the liminal experience.

I noted above that the liminal condition can be an openness to the new. But when the new identity of Asian Americans as a synthesis of the Asian and American worlds is not celebrated but considered often as inferior by the larger American society, how can these Asian Americans feel encouraged to welcome their new identity? Self-hatred will often be the result.

I also noted that liminality is conducive to community. But the dominant group would not leave their structure and join the Asian American strangers in the wilderness of liminal in-betweenness. White racism makes Asian American strangers even more reluctant to venture out of their ethnic enclaves. Liminality is certainly promoted when self-consciously liminal Asian Americans gather together. But realities of American society today certainly do not encourage Asian Americans to embrace their liminal wilderness experience. They are more often tempted either to cling unrealistically to their ethnic roots or to be oblivious to their ethnic past and live in the illusion that they are "Americans." The possibility of using their liminality as an opportunity to venture outside of Asian American ethnic enclaves and of trying to forge *communitas* with people across racial and ethnic lines certainly does not receive much encouragement and usually remains unfulfilled.

The third creative potential of liminality is its conducive nature to the attainment of a critical and prophetic insight about the center. But white racist hegemony sometimes leads Asian Americans and others at the edge to internalize the racist views of themselves and thus remain incapable of seeing the problems at the center. Even when some brave ones at the edge gain critical and prophetic insights, they are often not welcomed by either the American center, which only wants to protect the status quo, or the Asian center, which does not want anybody to rock the boat. In short, my proposal for an understanding of Asian American theology's context is that Asian Americans are in the predicament of "coerced liminality"—a potentially creative in-betweenness that is suppressed, frustrated, and unfulfilled by barriers that are not in one's own control. The Asian American minority in America, in other words, are a liminal people who can exercise their liminal creativity precisely to struggle against marginalization. But the creative potentials of their liminality are made ineffective by the demoralizing consequences of marginalization, and are crying out to be freed.

Chapter 2

GOD'S STRATEGIC ALLIANCE WITH THE LIMINAL AND MARGINALIZED

The good news of the Christian faith for liminal and marginalized Asian Americans is that the liminal place of marginality is precisely where God is to be found. God chooses the liminal margins of this world as the strategic place to begin God's decisive work of carrying out God's own end in creation. God chooses to work through liminal/ marginalized people in order to love and redeem all fallen humanity. This is because marginalized people, though sinful themselves, possess a more heightened liminality than those at the dominant centers of the world and thus a little more openness to God's good news. There is a passage in the fourth chapter of Matthew's Gospel that is seldom referred to in theology and preaching. After mentioning that Jesus settled and made his home in Capernaum by the sea, "in the territory of Zebulun and Naphatali [i.e., Galilee]," the author of Matthew quotes from Isaiah 9:1-2:

> Land of Zebulun, land of Naphtali,
>   on the road by the sea, across the Jordan,
>   Galilee of the Gentiles—
> the people who sat in darkness
>   have seen a great light,
> and for those who sat in the region

> and shadow of death
> light has dawned. (Matt. 4:15-16)

"A great light" in the "Galilee of the Gentiles"? "Light has dawned" in the land of "impure" people who are either Gentiles or those who associate with foreigners, the region of culturally and religiously backward peasants? No wonder the attention soon centered on Jerusalem as the center of the Christian movement while Galilee became invisible. The Gospels, however, point to Galilee as the place of Jesus' life and ministry. My thesis in this book is this: the redemption of fallen creation, especially humankind, involves the transformation of fallen humanity into persons who can participate in God's own work of repeating in time and space the inner-trinitarian community of love. For this purpose, the Son of God came into the world and appealed first to Galileans, a liminal and marginalized people who, unlike those at the centers, would be more open to the radical newness of the gospel. The Son of God made, in other words, a strategic alliance with Galileans and called them to be his own "first responders" or "first followers" in order to redeem ultimately the whole humankind.

God "could not" begin this work of redemption with the proud people at the dominant centers because their self-preoccupation is protective of the status quo. So God chose to approach first the liminal and marginalized people of the world. It is not that God loves them any more than the people at the centers. It is, rather, that to begin with marginalized people is more strategic for God because of their intensified liminality. It is the social location of liminality characteristic of marginalized people that makes it strategic for God to begin with them in God's work of redeeming all people. Healing and freeing up a marginalized people's suppressed liminal creativity is the first step God takes in God's grand project to build a beloved community here on earth.

Those who hear and respond to God's call to participate in God's own project in time and space, regardless of their ethnic or racial backgrounds, are chosen by God. But marginalized people, like Asian Americans and all others who may intentionally become liminal, are chosen by God in an additional sense—namely, in being called to become the first believers or initial responders. Asian American Christians' special calling, therefore, is God's appeal to them to exercise the creative openness of their suppressed liminality for the sake of the values of God's reign. It is worth repeating that this special calling is not limited to any one ethnic group. Any person who intentionally becomes liminal for the sake of God's kingdom has this special vocation. Asian Americans are simply *de facto* in the social location of liminality and marginality. Their calling is to be empowered by Christ to face up to and begin exercising their liminal creativity for God's reign.

God's strategic alliance with the liminal and marginalized began with God's choice of the nomadic family of Abraham. God called them to leave home and enter the life of liminality in the wilderness where they were to search for "a better country" whose "architect and builder is God" (Heb. 11:16, 10). God brought the already marginalized Hebrew slaves out of Egypt and threw them into a wilderness. In that harsh and liminal predicament, the liberated Hebrew slaves often despaired. But by God's unfailing care and presence, they experienced the emergence of *communitas* and solidarity as a people, as well as the birth of the monotheistic devotion to Yahweh who brought them out of the land of Egypt. In the wilderness experience, as biblical scholar Robert L. Cohn puts it, "the forces of liminality and communitas oxygenat[ed] the heavy atmosphere of structure." Cohn continues, "the religious and social values developed during this 'moment in and out of time' continued to reassert themselves in later periods . . . especially during the exile."[1] In this way, the history of Israel can be read as the story of God's choice of a liminal/marginalized people for God's own purposes and God's repeatedly empowering them to face up to, and to use creatively, their experiences of liminal wilderness and exile, or what Walter Brueggemann calls "landlessness." In Jesus of Nazareth, God's alliance with the liminal/marginalized takes the form of God's becoming a liminal/marginalized person Godself. God does God's redemptive work not just for the people but also as one among them. Crucially, God's incarnation as a historical person has to be taken in all of its concrete historicity. God did not become a general human being but a liminal/marginalized person. And God did not become a general marginalized person (who can only be found in a dictionary), but a concrete marginalized person—namely, a Galilean from the village of Nazareth. This means that Jesus was part of the religious, cultural, and political ethos of Galilee.

Thus, Jesus Christ, whom the Christian church confesses as Lord and Savior, is the Son of God who came *to* Galilee as well as *out of* Galilee. God, in other words, came to the world as a liminal/marginalized Galilean and also emerged out of the liminal/marginalized Galilee. A Christology that is faithful both to Jesus' historicity and to the church's confession must be both a descending and an ascending Christology. The bifurcation between what we call "Christology from below" and "Christology from above" must be overcome. I now turn to a consideration of Jesus Christ as a liminal/marginalized Galilean and the meaning of this Christ for Asian Americans and all other liminal/marginalized people.

GALILEE AS THE PLACE OF JESUS' MINISTRY AND GALILEANS AS HIS FIRST FOLLOWERS

The importance of Galilee, or more specifically the lower Galilee at the northern end of the Sea of Galilee, as the center of Jesus' ministry began to be noticed in the 1930s through the writings of Ernst Lohmeyer and R. H. Lightfoot.[2] Since then, their main thesis in regard to the opposition between Galilee as the place of people's acceptance of Jesus and Jerusalem as the city of hostile forces against him has received much development and refinement.[3] Most recently, the publication of several landmark studies on Galilee by Richard Horsley and others has added a great depth to our understanding of Galilee in its historical, sociological, and religious context.[4] The cumulative insight of these studies is the incontrovertible centrality of Galilee and Galileans in the New Testament Gospels' accounts of Jesus' life and teaching.

First, Galilee was the place where Jesus by divine intention lived and began his ministry. Matthew points to the divine intention in Jesus' choice of residence by referring to the dream that told Joseph to avoid Judea and to settle in Galilee (Matt. 2:22-23). Matthew cites the Old Testament to validate Jesus' move from Nazareth to Capernaum at the beginning to his ministry (Matt. 4:15-16; Isa. 9:1-2). Sean Freyne observes that for Matthew Galilee and Capernaum are not "just safe haven for the main character . . . ; they are actually the divinely willed theatres for the career of Jesus." Further, the description of Galilee as the "Galilee of the Gentiles," for Freyne, is in accord with Matthew's final attitude toward the Gentiles and Jesus' mission. Freyne concludes: "Galilee, therefore, has been blessed with a messianic visitation in the career of Jesus, seen as a light for those in darkness."[5] For Matthew and Mark, Jesus' first public appearance is his baptism by John, and both evangelists make a particular note that "Jesus came from [Nazareth of] Galilee" (Matt. 3:13; Mark 1:9)—to be baptized. At the moment of baptism, the voice from heaven declares, "This is ['You are,' Mark 1:11; Luke 3:22] my Son, the beloved, with whom I am well pleased" (Matt. 3:17). The words *this* and *you* here do not refer to some general or abstract human being but, rather, to "Jesus who came from Galilee," Jesus the Galilean. That the ensuing drama is about the Galilean Jesus and that this is God's own intention is unmistakably noted by the evangelists. After Jesus' baptism as a Galilean and his temptations in the wilderness, it is in Galilee that he inaugurates his main teaching: "Repent, for the kingdom of heaven has come near" (Matt. 4:17).

Second, Capernaum in the lower Galilee was the headquarters of Jesus' ministry, and Jesus received the greatest acceptance in Galilee. Matthew and Mark report that at the very beginning of Jesus' ministry he "went throughout Galilee," teaching and healing people (Matt. 4:23; Mark 1:39). Those from outside of Galilee such as Judea, Jerusalem,

Idumea, Tyre, and Sidon also came to hear Jesus but, as Mark emphasizes, it was the Galilean followers who were a "great multitude" (Mark 3:7-8). Jesus travels to the surrounding Gentile territories but always returns to Galilee (Mark 7:31).

Usually, according to all four Gospels, Judea, or more particularly Jerusalem, is the place of rejection while Galilee is the place of acceptance and refuge. In John 3, Jesus goes to the "Judean countryside" (v. 22), but when he hears that the Pharisees are alarmed about him, Jesus "left Judea and started back to Galilee" (John 4:1-3). And, "when he came to Galilee, the Galileans welcomed him" (John 4:45). The people at the center of the religious establishment were not the ones who recognized and accepted the Word become flesh (John 1); rather, the despised people of Galilee were those who welcomed the Messiah.

The Galilean acceptance of Jesus was not unqualified. Matthew and Luke record Jesus' severe judgment of Chorazin, Bethsaida, and even Capernaum for their lack of repentance. Unlike John, the Synoptic Gospels have Jesus use the proverbial saying, "Prophets are not without honor except in their own country," in regard to the incident of rejection in Nazareth (Matt. 13:54-58; Mark 6:1-6a; Luke 4:16-30). Mark comments that Jesus "was amazed at their unbelief" (6:6a). Peter's denial of Jesus, the male disciples' absence at the crucifixion, and other incidents all point to the fallibility of Jesus' Galilean followers. The Gospels' record of the fallibility of Jesus' disciples and the nonresponse from some Galileans keep us from any kind of romanticism about Galilee. Galileans were sinful just as anyone else. As Freyne points out, however, in comparison to the hostility of Jerusalem to Jesus, the warmth of the Galilean acceptance of him is overwhelming. Galileans in their liminal predicament had a greater openness to the new message of Jesus than those at the center did. Although Jesus' Galilean followers were not perfect disciples, they still were Jesus' most loyal friends. At the time of Jesus' agonizing death on the cross, Galilee did not totally abandon him. As Matthew records, "Many women were also there, looking on from a distance; they had followed Jesus from

Galilee and had provided for him" (27:55). Galilee was with Jesus at his burial. "The women who had come with him from Galilee followed, and they saw the tomb and how his body was laid. Then they returned, and prepared spices and ointments" (Luke 23:55-56). Galilee did not leave him alone in his death, as again the women from Galilee went to the tomb with spices to anoint him (Matt. 28:1; Mark 16:1; Luke 24:1; John 20:1). Thus, even among Jesus' Galilean followers, the women were the most faithful. In this way, the faithfulness of the women from Galilee connects Jesus' Galilean ministry before the crucifixion with the resurrected Jesus who reunites with the disciples in Galilee. Jesus reaffirms his initial choice of Galilee as his place of work by telling his disciples ahead of time: "But after I am raised up, I will go ahead of you to Galilee" (Matt. 26:32). At the dawn of the Easter morning, an angel in lightning white tells Mary Magdalene and "the other Mary" that Jesus "has been raised from the dead, and indeed he is going ahead of you to Galilee; there you will see him" (Matt. 28:7; Mark 16:7). In Matthew's account, Jesus himself appears and tells the women: "Do not be afraid; go and tell my brothers to go to Galilee; there they will see me" (Matt. 28:10). A few verses later, we are told that the eleven disciples "went to Galilee, to the mountain to which Jesus had directed them" and that there "they saw him." And the risen Jesus with "all the authority in heaven and on earth" gives his Galilean disciples on this Galilean mountain the great commission to spread the gospel to "all the nations" (Matt. 28:16-19).

So the reunion of the risen Jesus with his Galilean disciples happens not in Jerusalem, the center of religious establishment, but in Galilee, the peripheral area that is scorned by the center. Galilee is the place of the disciples' "seeing" of the resurrection. In this way, the risen Jesus relates himself to what he did in Galilee: his ministry in which "the blind receive their sight, the lame walk, the lepers are cleansed, the deaf hear, the dead are raised, the poor have the good news brought to them" (Luke 7:22). The one who turns out to be stronger than death is not any ruler or high priest at the religious and political center of Jerusalem but, rather, Jesus of Nazareth in Galilee who epitomized in his life the reign of God's compassion, forgiveness, and justice. And the place where the disciples experience this fact is Galilee. Galilee is Jesus' chosen place for his ministry both before and after the resurrection.

Luke reports in Acts 1 that Galileans were the witnesses to Jesus' ascension. As Jesus "was lifted up," "two men in white robes" said: "Men of Galilee, why do you stand looking up toward heaven? This Jesus, who has been taken up from you into heaven, will come in the same way as you saw him go into heaven" (v. 11). Galileans are those who are given the secret of how Jesus was going to return. Galileans appear again in Acts 2, as Luke records Jesus' Galilean followers, commissioned by God to spread the good news to "all nations," beginning to fulfill their role as the "first responders" to Jesus. As a group of Jesus' followers began speaking in tongues about "God's deeds of power" (v. 11), the Jews "from every nation under heaven living in Jerusalem" gathered near them and were "bewildered, because each one heard them speaking in the native tongue of each." They asked: "Are not all these who are speaking Galileans?" (vv. 5-7). Thus, in choosing Galilee as the primary place of Jesus' ministry, God's ultimate intention went far beyond Galilee.

Thus far, we have looked through the texts of the Synoptic Gospels, the Fourth Gospel, and Acts as they are given in the New Testament canon. Some scholars have tried to work with the oldest materials in order to get a picture of the earliest followers of Jesus and their communities (that is, what has been called the "Jesus Movement") in Jesus' own time and soon after the resurrection. Most recently, Richard A. Horsley, in his book *Sociology and the Jesus Movement*, analyzed the Q material (the sayings source found in both Matthew and Luke but not in Mark) as well as the text of Mark itself. Horsley's conclusion is that "the arena of Jesus' activity is primarily Galilee," and that much of the materials in the Gospels, including "Q" and Mark, were probably developed in Galilee or southern Syria. The Q people, according to Horsley, "understand John and Jesus as the climactic figures in the line of the prophets, who almost by definition, stood over against and were rejected by the ruling institutions and their representatives [i.e., Jerusalem]." Horsley notes further that "the only place names [in Q], apart from the doomed Jerusalem, are towns at the northern end of the Sea of Galilee, Capernaum, Chorazin, and Bethsaida." In short, "the social location [of Jesus and the Jesus Movement] is popular culture, apparently Galilean, remote from Temple and official tradition." An examination of the earliest materials confirms, then, what we saw in the Gospels as a whole, namely, "that Galilee, as opposed to Jerusalem, was Jesus' chosen arena of ministry, and that primarily Galileans constituted Jesus first followers or the participants in the 'Jesus Movement.'"[6]

THE LIMINALITY OF GALILEE AND GALILEANS

What is the meaning of God's appeal to Galilee and the Galileans? Why Galilee, and why Galileans? I have already suggested that God's choice of Galilee as Jesus' place of ministry is due to the limited and yet real openness of Galileans as a liminal/marginalized people. But in what ways were Galilee as a place and Galileans as a people both liminal and also marginalized? An understanding of Galilee's liminal marginality is crucial for Asian American theology because such an understanding shows concretely the ways in which the social location of Jesus relates to the social location of Asian Americans. Moreover, the way Jesus dealt with his own social location can teach Asian Americans how to deal with theirs.

Biblical scholars have noted the liminal character of Galilee and Galileans although they do not use the term *liminality*. I cite here just a few examples. Sean Freyne, for example, concludes his literary and historical study of Galilee by suggesting that the Gospel narratives "use Galilee as a symbol of the periphery becoming the new, non-localized center of divine presence." Freyne mentions Galilee's "detachment" and "distance" from the center of power in Jerusalem that made Galileans more "open" for Jesus' ministry.[7] L. E. Elliott-Binns also suggests that Galilee's freer atmosphere and its distance from the capital might have been the reasons for Jesus' choice of Galilee as the center of his ministry. Anne Hennessy, still another biblical scholar, refers to Galilee as an "open space" and a land of a "broader range of experiences" and "accessible horizons" as the reasons for Galilee's importance in Jesus' ministry.[8]

The terms *open space*, *detachment*, *freer atmosphere*, and *periphery* all refer to a liminal situation. In what follows, I shall briefly outline the situation of Galilee and Galileans as possessing the creative potentials of liminal space. First of all, Galilee's geographical location has a great deal to do with its political and social and cultural liminality.[9] The Hebrew term *ha-galil* is a secondary shortening of an original *galil-hagoyim*, meaning "circle of peoples" or "circle of the nations" (Isa. 9:1; quoted in Matt. 4:15, translated into English as "Galilee of the Gentiles"). Thus, the name *Galilee* refers to the geographical and political reality of being surrounded by powerful nations and empires and being frequently subjected to their infiltration, migration, and domination. From 734 B.C.E. on through the next six centuries, Galilee was under the foreign administration of Assyrians, Babylonians, Persians, Macedonians, Egyptians, and Syrians. Galilee in Jesus' time was a conquered territory of Rome. It is important to note here that the administration of Galilee by foreign powers usually did not involve any deployment of native Galileans. Assyrians ruled Galilee directly from their city of Megiddo. The Hellenistic empires of the Ptolemies and Seleucids and later the Hasmonean high-priestly regime followed by the Romans all used the Galilean city of Sepphoris as their administrative and military center, until the Roman client-ruler Antipas built Tiberius as the second foreign administrative city in Galilee. But the officialdom in Sepphoris and Tiberius was peopled not by native Galileans but by foreigners brought in from outside of Galilee. As Horsley explains, Galilee, in contrast to Samaria and Judea, did not have its own native aristocracy that could rule its own people on behalf of the foreign powers and function as a kind of buffer, thereby mitigating, at least in some ways, the harsh impact of foreign domination.[10]

The direct rule of Galilee by the foreign conquerors made it difficult for Galileans to develop any official tradition out of its popular customs or any clear sense of themselves as a political power or an ethnic group. Horsley notes that from the earliest times "in the experience of Israel as a political power, the Galilean tribes must have been somewhat peripheral."[11] Galilee was a "frontier" for the encircling foreign powers as well as for the power center of Israel in Jerusalem. The political and religious centers of the Israelites were always in the south at Shilo, Gilgal, Shechem, and then Jerusalem, while no central city or temple was established by the indigenous people of Galilee. Being, therefore, a "power vacuum," Galilee lacked any political and cultural coherence or unity as a region.[12] Galilee was geographically, politically, and culturally a relatively unstructured frontier land. Galilee was at the edge, in-between, out of the power structure, and thus liminal. Galilee was liminal also due to its cultural diversity. The repeated foreign invasions exposed Galileans to the existence of different cultures. Although the outsiders living in Sepphoris and Tiberius had only minimal contact with Galilean villagers, there would still have been what Horsley calls a "steady and slow" cultural impact upon Galileans. Galilean population itself was also mixed. In 732 B.C.E., the Assyrian conqueror Tiglath-pileser took as many as 13,520 Galilean prisoners to Assyria, seriously depopulating Galilee. Scholars believe that Galilee was probably resettled largely by non-Israelites in Persian and Hellenistic times. So non-Israelites and "Gentiles" lived alongside Galilean villagers. Horsley reports, "Within the same village, Israelites and Gentiles lived in adjacent houses or shared the same courtyard, or perhaps even shared a house or oven."[13]

Another factor that broadened the cultural outlook of Galileans was the presence of international trade routes. For example, Capernaum, the headquarters of Jesus' ministry, was near the border between

Galilee and Golan. Located near a border crossing, Capernaum surely must have been affected by the foreign people in transit. Galilee, therefore, was culturally a frontier. Galilee was liminal.

Third, Galilee was religiously liminal. Galileans felt themselves as both belonging to the religious center, the Jerusalem Temple, and also distant from it. To understand the relation between Galilee and Jerusalem, we must recall that Galilee and Judea were under different foreign administrations for eight centuries, with the result that Galileans and Judeans underwent separate developments in their religious lives. Moreover, Judeans, unlike Galileans, had many centuries to get adjusted to the Temple-state rule, and had their own aristocracy and priestly elites who could in some ways "soften" the brunt of the foreign rule through the Temple-state structure. Galilee, on the other hand, had no sacred center of its own or religious establishment and thus maintained its own inherited religious beliefs and customs in their popular forms. Therefore, when Galilee came under the jurisdiction of Jerusalem in the early Roman period, only about one hundred years before the time of Jesus, the Temple-based high-priestly structure must have appeared to Galileans as odd versions of their ancient Israelite tradition. Galileans, especially those with an Israelite background, might have found Jerusalem's religious establishment as the new political and economic center of power strange and disagreeable. Galileans worshiped the same God of Israel and shared with the Jerusalem Temple establishment common religious roots. They both shared the exodus story, the Mosaic covenant, stories of independent early Israel prior to the Solomonic monarchy and its temple, the Elijah-Elisha story cycle, the Song of Deborah, and others. Some Galileans, therefore, can be assumed to have had some genuine loyalty to Jerusalem. Some even made pilgrimages to the Temple, although how many made such pilgrimages is uncertain.[14]

So Galileans' position in relation to Jerusalem was one of ambivalence. Galileans felt both belonging to Jerusalem and at the same time detached from it. They were liminal in their relation to the Jerusalem

Temple-state. From this liminal space, Galileans had the capacity to see the center with a critical eye.

THE MARGINALIZATION OF GALILEE AND GALILEANS

Galileans were not just left alone in their liminal situation but were oppressed, dehumanized, and looked down upon. Galileans were marginalized by the foreign invaders and also by the religious-political center, the Jerusalem Temple-state. As noted earlier, Galilee was repeatedly invaded and exploited by various foreign empires throughout its history. Foreign conquerors and their agents were also in their midst within Galilee, in Sepphoris and later Tiberius.

Galilee was also politically vulnerable to the center of power within Israel itself. When King Solomon was building the Temple, for example, all Israel was forced to generate revenues and forced labor, but Galilee was affected most severely. In order to solve a "balance of payments" problem, Solomon ceded to Hiram, king of Tyre, "twenty cities in the land of Galilee"—along with their people, of course—in payment (1 Kgs. 9:10-14). Galilean peasants were mere dispensable pawns to the center of power.[15]

Galileans were also objects of scorn within Israel, especially in the eyes of the Jews in Jerusalem, for cultural and religious "backward-ness." Galileans were despised for their lack of knowledge of the Torah and for their laxness in following the law and in paying taxes. Galileans were looked down upon because they were considered culturally impure due to their associations with foreigners. Galileans were also jeered at because they did not speak correct Aramaic.

But most demoralizing and destructive for Galilean peasants was their economic exploitation by the Jerusalem Temple-state and their consequent social and religious alienation. Under Herodian client-kings, Galileans villagers were forced to pay three layers of taxes: the dues to Temple and priests, tribute to Rome, and taxes to Herod,

Antipas, and Agrippas. It has been estimated that over one-third of Galilean peasants' crops was taken in order to meet the three different demands.[16] When Antipas launched the projects of rebuilding Sepphoris and of building Tiberius, the exploitation of Galilean peasantry became intensified. Invariably, the peasants lapsed in meeting the demands and began incurring debts. When they were unable to pay back debts, they lost their land and became tenants for their creditors. Often they left their ancestral homes in search of work. This downward spiral of indebtedness had at least three consequences. The first is the shift in their social position. Galileans who lost their lands now occupied a less respectable social position as sharecroppers or laborers, often on what had been their own ancestral land. Such a forced downward mobility certainly must have been deeply demoralizing. The second consequence was the disintegration of the fundamental social forms of family and village community. Many became day laborers or had to leave home in search of work, while some others joined bands of brigands. Galileans were suffering a serious social dislocation and disruption.

Perhaps the most agonizing consequence of Galileans' economic plight was religious in nature. The Jerusalem Temple stipulated that the productivity and fertility of the land were tied to the peasants' faithful fulfillment of the thank-offerings and other Temple dues and tithes. Any lapse in these payments meant a breach not only of a financial kind but also of a religious nature. Not to pay dues to the Temple was not to fulfill a religious obligation. With the relationship with the Temple broken, the peasants found themselves separated from the only place where they could pray for God's blessings of the fertility and productivity of their land, which in turn would be the only way through which they could hope for a better crop and for the restoration of their relationship with the Temple.[17] When Jesus taught his disciples to pray for the forgiveness of their "debts," he had both real financial indebtedness and also something much more crucial in mind.

The dominant center's marginalization of Galileans would have frustrated, suppressed, and disabled the creative potential of Galileans' liminality. The creative thrust of their liminality was of course never completely dormant but was expressed in the form of what political scientist James C. Scott calls "subtle acts of resistance" as well as in the appearance of armed bandits. Banditry is always a form of protest to oppression. But what banditry usually lacks is "a vision of a different social order that one might aspire to." And the oppressed people's rebellious actions only led to a greater suppression by the center, thereby creating a "spiral of violence."[18]

Galileans needed to be empowered to resist marginalization. They needed someone to help them break the spiral of violence and restore peace in the land. Galilee needed to be healed and redirected in the exercise of their liminal creativity. They needed a radically new vision of how human relatedness could be changed. They needed to be empowered to exercise their liminal creativity.

Galileans got far more than they could ever have hoped for. God came to dwell among them to heal and transform them and to empower them to exercise their liminal powers in the way they were intended to be exercised. They were given a new vision of God's "new family" with Jesus as the head. What is more, God came to them to invite them to be the "first responders" to the new vision. They would in turn proclaim what God had done for them to others in the world.

Asian Americans' predicament in the United States is similar to that of the Galileans of the first century. God comes to Asian Americans again today in the form of Jesus Christ who will heal us and empower us. We now need to examine carefully how and for what this Jesus, a liminal/marginalized person, exercised his liminal creativity and how God in him was the forgiving, saving, and enabling God for the liminal/marginalized Galileans. We need to see why the hope of Asian Americans lies in the Galilean Jesus and the God who was in him.

Chapter 3
GOD AND LIMINALITY

In this chapter, I turn to the fundamental framework of the Asian American theology that I have been articulating. What God is ultimately aiming at in creating the world and in God's providential rule needs to be spelled out so that the ultimate meaning of what I say regarding God's redemptive work and Christian discipleship may be clear.

Second, it is important to understand how God's entrance into a liminal space in Jesus Christ is rooted in a liminality within God's internal life and being. By speaking about the immanent Trinity as the foundation of God's activity in history, one may affirm that what God does in history is not incidental to God but is grounded in the very nature of God's own being and life.

Speaking about these most basic matters is not to engage in a speculative, deductive, or "from above" kind of theology that says things about history and human life on the basis of certain abstract presuppositions which are removed from concrete historical process. What I say about God's end in creation and God's internal life is actually read off of God's actions in history—most centrally, in the life, work, death, and resurrection of Jesus Christ as reread in light of the concrete context of Asian Americans. Although I do not explicitly deal with the question of how the doctrine of God is "read off" of God's actions of history, in discussing the way of Jesus the Galilean as the Christ I will deal with the material that is the basis for articulating the doctrine of God's internal life.

GOD'S END IN CREATION

Jonathan Edwards's conception of the end or purpose for which God created the world provides the ultimate meaning of his understanding of all that God does in human history. I borrow Edwards's understanding of God's end in creation as the temporal repetition of God's inner-trinitarian communion, because it comports well with Asian American theology's need to spell out how marginalized and liminal Asian Americans can attain a life of belonging and communion in America.

Edwards's conception of God's end in creation must be understood in conjunction with his highly original formulation of the being of God as at once fully actual and also inherently disposed to increase in actuality. The exercise of the divine disposition in God's knowing or loving represents the movement from the possibility of that to which the disposition is disposed, to the actuality of that possibility. Thus, the exercise of disposition results in an ontological increase.

For Edwards, God's essence is the eternal disposition to bring about and delight in communal love and beauty, and this disposition is fully and perfectly exercised within God's internal life. God in God's internal being, therefore, is all that God has to be in order to be God. God's internal "fullness" is the full actuality of the divine being plus an infinite increase of that being within God's own being. God's self-communication among the Trinity, Edwards says, is the full actualization of the divine being that is "completely equal to" the eternal disposition. There is no lack in God's actuality as God.[1]

God is actual. However, God also remains essentially the eternal disposition to bring about and delight in communal love and beauty. The paradoxical truth is that in God actuality and disposition coincide. Now, the question is, How can the divine disposition that is fully exercised within the Trinity be further exercised? Edwards's answer is *ad extra*, that is, outside of God's internal being.

God creates the world, according to Edwards, so that God's dispositional essence could now be exercised outside of God's internal fullness. But a question arises: Anything that God aims at must be the highest good, and God alone is the highest good. But if God as the highest good is fully actual within God's own being, what could be the end God could aim at in exercising God's disposition outside of Godself? Edwards's answer to this question is: God's internal fullness itself "repeated" in time and space.[2] The world is to be a repetition of God's internal being. Since the world is a "repetition" of God's prior actuality, God's perfection in actuality is safeguarded. But "repetition" also is something that happens in time and space. So the notion of repetition protects God's prior perfection and at the time bestows an ontological significance to what God does in time and space. Since God's internal beauty of being is infinite, its repetition in time and space will take an "everlasting" time through the eschaton and into the unending time in heaven. The world will have true and real repetitions of God's beauty in time and space, but will never be a complete "increase" of God's internal being. The "repetition" or "increase" continues for an everlasting duration. Therefore, the God–world distinction will never be abolished.[3]

Edwards's achievement is that he is able to see God as involved in time without subjecting God's prior actuality to temporal process. God's repetition in time and space of God's intra-trinitarian communion is achieved through the sanctified human being's loving communion with God and with others. What human beings do in time and space can be a participation in God's own work of repeating in time God's internal communion. In short, Asian American theology can appropriate Edwards's notion that one's primary task in following Christ is to help establish loving communion with others and that striving for such a goal is nothing less than a participation in God's own work in history.

LIMINALITY IN GOD

The Christian faith affirms that Jesus Christ is the incarnate Son of God. What Jesus is is what God is, and what Jesus does is what God does. In Jesus the Galilean, we meet God Godself, not some representative of God and not some God-like being. If this were not so, our salvation wrought in Jesus Christ would not be salvation from God Godself.

So when Jesus the Galilean chose the liminal and marginalized Galilee as the place of his ministry, God Godself was making this choice. When Jesus lived the life of a liminal and marginalized Galilean, God Godself lived a liminal and marginalized human life. If this is the case, then do the incarnate Son of God's liminality and marginalization correspond to any aspect of God's internal life as God? If Jesus is God Godself, there must be at least liminality in God. There must be liminality in God as the basis of Jesus' liminality and as the possibility of marginalization here on earth.

Marginalization, unlike liminality, is not what Jesus willed for himself. Marginalization is part of the fallen condition of God's creation and, as such, cannot be rooted in God's own inner life. Nevertheless, there must be something in God's own being that is the ground of the possibility of Jesus' act of taking marginalization upon himself. Liminality in God is the ground of the possibility that God in time may participate in the condition of being marginalized.

One enters liminality by leaving behind for a moment his or her structure and status. Liminality is the room into which one is ready to let the other come as the other. Liminality is receptivity and thus also vulnerability. Liminality as a means of God's expression of God's love for the other, therefore, is also God's "capacity" to take marginalization and even death upon Godself, as God did in Jesus the incarnate Son.

Is Jonathan Edwards's conception of God's intra-trinitarian life capable of accommodating liminality? Liminality among the persons of the Trinity is really a further elaboration of the distinction between them. To the extent that Edwards, as the theological tradition itself, affirms a real distinction between the persons, his doctrine of the Trinity, in my view, is capable of accommodating liminality. Edwards wrote, "If God beholds himself so as hence to have delight and joy in himself, he must become his own object: there must be a duplicity." Further, "And I suppose the Deity to be truly and properly repeated by God's thus having an idea of himself . . . and that by this means the Godhead is truly generated and repeated."[4] Edwards's insistence that there must be a "duplicity" between the Father and the Son can be taken to mean that there is a real otherness and a "distance" between them, and the Father delights in and loves the Son as truly Other. This otherness and distance between the Father and the Son are the liminal space between them. The Father out of love for the Son enters into a liminal space in meeting the Son. Out of the liminal space between them emerges (proceeds) the communion of the Father and the Son—namely, the Holy Spirit.

What I am claiming in the above interpretation is only that placing liminality in the intra-trinitarian life at least would not be inconsistent with Edwards's actual exposition of the Trinity. For an articulation of liminality in the Trinity in a quite clear fashion (though without actually using the term "liminality"), I turn to the conception of the Trinity in Hans Urs von Balthasar's theology.

In theologies utilizing substance-metaphysics, such as Thomas Aquinas's doctrine of God, there is an emphasis upon divine immutability and simplicity. Within such a theology, there are limitations upon conceiving the relations among the three persons of the Trinity in a dynamic way. But in a theology that is informed by dynamic ontologies of love, it is easier to conceive of God's inner life as involving movements, processes, and transitions. Hans Urs von Balthasar's theology, just as that of Jonathan Edwards, is a fine example of such a dynamic and relational perspective. I believe von Balthasar's conceptions of the Father's self-emptying (kenotic) act of begetting the Son and of the mutual relation between the Father and the Son provide insights that support our claim that there is liminality within God's inner-trinitarian life.

According to von Balthasar, the Father's generation of the Son is an act of complete self-giving to the Son. Von Balthasar writes:

> We shall never know how to express the abyss-like depths of the Father's self-giving . . . [which is] an eternal "super-kenosis." . . . Everything that can be thought and imagined where God is concerned is, in advance, included and transcended in this self-destitution which constitutes the Person of the Father, and at the same time, those of the Son and the Spirit.[5]

In generating the Son, the Father gives over the divine substance in such a manner that, in handing it over to the Son, according to von Balthasar, the Father nevertheless retains it at the same time.[6]

Von Balthasar characterizes the Father's "self-giving" also as " 'letting-go' of his divinity," "self-surrender," and "stripping" himself of his Godhead.[7] This self-giving is the expression of the Father's love for the Son and as such constitutes the Father's being as the first person of the Trinity. Von Balthasar's language about the Father "not grasp[ing] the divinity" corresponds to Paul's words in Philippians: "[Christ,] though he was in the form of God, did not regard equality with God as something to be exploited" (Phil. 2:6). The Father's "original kenosis" also corresponds to Jesus' experience of being "forsaken" by God on the cross (Mark 15:34).

Now, liminality is a space in which one is out of structure by being freed from one's status, role, and place in the hierarchy. The Father's not grasping his divine status by completely giving it to the Son, then, places the Father in a liminal space, just as Christ's not grasping his being in the "form of God" puts him in a liminal condition. The Father's love of the Son that leads the Father to empty himself for the Son places the Father in an "abyss," which is again a liminal space.

According to von Balthasar, the Father does not create a clone of himself in generating the Son but, rather, brings into being a genuine Other with all the otherness entailed in an other. The Son is the Father's Thou, "infinitely Other," with all the autonomy of freedom required of a distinct person. In generating this Son out of love, according to von Balthasar, the Father posits "an infinite distance" between himself and the Son. This distance is a necessity in order to maintain "the personal peculiarity in the being and acting of each Person."[8] Of course, the Father is always with the Son out of love, but at the same time, and also out of love, the Father withdraws from the Son and maintains the personal distance. This distance between the Father and the Son, according to von Balthasar, is the ultimate ground of the distance the incarnate Son experiences from the Father on the cross.[9]

Von Balthasar further characterizes the Father's generation of the Son out of love as an act of "leaving-free" the Son. This "leaving-free" the Son involves the Father's allowing "an area for his unique personal mode of divine autonomy." The Father's withdrawal from the Son allows for "a mode of glory distinctive to the Son's mode of being God."[10] The Father, according to von Balthasar, is of course always in the Son out of love, but at the same time the Father withdraws from the Son out of love as well as out of respect for the Son's free choice to give himself completely back to the Father. Margaret Turek sums up von Balthasar's point, as she writes, "God the Father is the 'greater' One who not only 'makes space' for filial freedom over against himself, but also remains hidden in this 'space' as the engendering source of the Son's ability to give himself in love."[11] By implication, then, the Son also gives himself to the Father out of love. And in doing so he experiences a leaving behind of his divine status, thereby placing himself in liminality. What occurs in the space of liminality that both the Father and the Son experience together von Balthasar clearly indicates in the following passage:

> The Father's act of surrender calls for its own area of free-dom; the Son's act, whereby he receives himself from and

acknowledges his indebtedness to the Father, requires its own area; and *the act whereby the Spirit proceeds, illuminating the most intimate love of Father and Son*, testifying to it and fanning it into flame, demands its own area of freedom. However intimate the relationship, it implies that the distinction between the persons is maintained. *Something like infinite "duration" [Dauer] and infinite "space" [Raum] must be attributed to the acts of reciprocal love so that the life of the* communio, *or fellowship, can develop*. . . . True, all temporal notions of "before" and "after" must be kept at a distance; but absolute freedom must provide the acting area [*Spiel-Raum*] in which it is to develop—and develop in terms of love and blessedness.[12]

It would not be far from the truth to say that von Balthasar could just as well have used the concept of liminality in the above discussion. The "acting area" and "room" in which the persons of the Trinity exercise their freedom is the space created by the persons' mutual acts of "letting the other be." It is a space to which the persons "withdraw" themselves. It is an open area in which new possibilities are allowed. It is a liminal space.

It should also be recalled that, according to Victor Turner, *communitas* or communion emerges out of the liminal space experienced together by two or more persons who are out of structure. And von Balthasar associates the Holy Spirit with the communal love that is generated from the liminal space experienced by the Father and the Son. Von Balthasar writes:

Inherent in the Father's love is an absolute renunciation: he will not be God for himself alone. He lets go of his divinity and, in this sense, manifests a (divine) God-lessness (of love, of course). . . . The Son's answer to the gift of Godhead (of equal substance with the Father) can only be eternal thanksgiving (*eucharistia*) to the Father, the Source—a thanksgiving as self-less and unreserved as the Father's original self-surrender. Proceeding from both, as their subsistent

"We," there breathes the "Spirit" who is common to both: as the essence of love, he maintains the infinite difference between them, seals it and, since he is the one Spirit of them both, bridges it.[13]

In sum, we can summarize von Balthasar's discussion of the Father's generation of the Son using the concept of liminality. As the Father's love moves him to give himself (while also remaining himself) to the Son, the Father moves into a liminal space by letting go of his divinity and his divine status (while also retaining them). As the Father withdraws from the Son (while also remaining in the Son), he allows an "action room" (*Spiel-Raum*) or a space of possibilities for the sake of the Son's being a genuine Other to the Father, that is, One who can exercise absolute freedom.

The Son also is the Son "only as he who utterly surrenders himself to the Father."[14] Out of the "abyss," "infinite distance," and what we would call "liminality," experienced by the Father and the Son together in their acts of loving self-surrender, emerges the *communitas* or communion of the Father and the Son, the person of the Holy Spirit.

What happens within the immanent Trinity is reflected in God's trinitarian acts of redemption in history. To speak about liminality within God's own life is to affirm that God's experiences of liminality in history are God's expression of God's own nature and being. What God does in history is not what God does *only* in history but is the way God is eternally and without which God would not be God.

THE INCARNATION AND LIMINALITY

Liminality belongs to the internal life of God. In a similar way, liminality also belongs to the order of creation and not to the forces that resist God's end in creation. The experience of liminality in human life is the way human community emerges; therefore, liminality in human existence is meant to be used in humanity's participation in, and contribution to, God's reaching the end for which God created the world:

namely, the repetition of the inner-trinitarian communion of love in time and space.

But humanity did not use liminality in this way, as the story of Adam and Eve tells us. Instead of facing the uncertainty and openness of liminality with faith and courage, human beings began to live by the idolatrous and prideful thought that they "will be like God, knowing good and evil" (Gen. 3:5). Instead of being open to the new ideas, human beings absolutized certain finite principles and condemned different ideas as false. Instead of forming community and solidarity through liminality, human beings clung to the human-made borders, living in an alienation from each other. Instead of providing the absolutized centers of societies a prophetic criticism from the liminal space, human beings joined with those at the dominant centers and became oppressive to those at the periphery. In these ways, human beings began to elude the challenge to face their liminal experiences and exercise the creative powers of liminality to promote God's project of repeating loving communion in human history.

In order to put humanity back on the track, so to speak, of participating in God's project, God first established a covenant with Israel, because the people of Israel as the nomadic children of Abraham lived in a situation of an accentuated liminality and were—at least in principle—more open to the new, capable of forming community, and prophetically critical of the status quo.

In God's incarnation in Jesus, the eternal Son became liminal in history itself. Just as God chose to work through the children of Israel in the days of the Old Testament, now in becoming incarnate in Jesus the Galilean, God became liminal in Jesus the Galilean and appealed first to Galileans because Galileans were living in an accentuated liminality. All human beings, in spite of their fallen condition, are capable of experiencing liminality. But Galileans were in a more explicit way liminal in the religious, political, sociocultural, and economic aspects of their lives. It was strategic, therefore, for God to become incarnate as a Galilean and appeal first to Galileans.

The incarnation, or God's becoming a Galilean human being, occurred when human beings became hopelessly fallen. But God's coming to the world in Jesus to redeem the world was in pursuance of the eternal covenant between God the Father and God the Son to redeem fallen humanity. This covenant in turn is rooted in the eternal love between the Father and the Son. Therefore, the incarnation is rooted in the way God is in God's very being.

The incarnate Son's (that is, the Galilean Jesus') liminality reached its climax in Jesus' death on the cross. The response that is appropriate for Galileans and other human beings would be for them to become personally conscious of their liminality and meet Jesus in his liminality on the cross. Out of the meeting of Jesus and sinful human beings in the liminal space of Jesus' cross, a transforming *communitas* would emerge in the power of the Holy Spirit, and God and the world would be reconciled (2 Cor. 5:19).

A loving communion between the incarnate Son and fallen humanity and the transformation of wayward human beings into a new existence began occurring in a decisive way through the ministry, death, and resurrection of Jesus Christ. But the completion of this work of the incarnate Son is eschatological.

So, through the incarnation, God the Son entered into human liminality because liminality belongs to the order of creation and is an inherent part of human existence. In Christ God became a marginalized Galilean human being because, in the words of Gregory of Nazianzus, "That which he has not assumed, he has not healed."[15] Jesus did not marginalize others, and he did not evade the human experiences of liminality even when that liminality was the liminality of death. However, he participated fully in the human predicament in the sense that he did not run away from becoming marginalized and oppressed by self-absolutizing humanity.

Chapter 4

THE WAY OF THE LIMINAL JESUS AS THE CHRIST

Like other Galileans, Jesus was liminal and marginalized. But he was different from other Galileans. In spite of the demoralizing effects of marginalization, Jesus was able to exercise the creative potentials of his liminality for God's end in creation. The realization of the reign of God is the actualization of God's end in creation. It should be noted here that Jesus did not exercise his liminality's creativity for some general purposes; rather, he did so for the specific purposes of bringing about on earth the reign of God. According to the New Testament, Jesus was both the embodiment and bringer of the reign of God.[1] Jesus' life and ministry were not devoted to the fulfillment of some anthropologically conceived creativity of liminality but, rather, to the utilization of liminality's creativity for God's own purposes for created existence. Theology in this way assigns a specific direction to the general potentials of liminality.

LEAVING HOME: JESUS' APPROPRIATION OF LIMINALITY

Scholars believe that Jesus' years of youth were probably quite uneventful and that he was settled in a household of a modest socioeconomic status. But sometime in his late twenties, perhaps around 28 C.E., Jesus

left home and his close family to lead a self-consciously liminal and marginalized life.[2] The event of Jesus' leaving home is seldom discussed in
studies of the historical Jesus. But for Asian Americans, many of whom
are immigrants or the children of immigrants, Jesus' departure from
home is significant. The Gospels also make it clear that this was not just
a casual event in Jesus' life.

For Jesus, leaving home, as it would be for any one in his circumstances, was an act with grave consequences. In his day the Galilean
household was the primary place of socialization, where a person's social
roles and their meanings were both learned and played out. Identity
did not exist apart from a person's household, kinship relations, and
village. For Jesus to leave his household, therefore, was to be cut off
from the place that had given him his identity. Leaving home meant
going out of the structure of one's life. It meant entering a wilderness,
a liminal space.[3]

Why did Jesus leave home? Was he not already liminal as a person
living in Galilee? We must here make a distinction between "objective
liminality," on the one hand, and "subjective liminality," on the other.
A person or a people may be objectively or *de facto* liminal ("objective liminality"), but may not be subjectively and personally aware of it
("subjective liminality"). A person in a liminal situation may not be exis-
tentially aware of his/her liminality for different reasons. He or she may
be refusing to face up to it and thus denying it, or his or her personal
circumstances may be such that he or she is kept away from becoming
personally aware of it. Galileans were objectively liminal but they were
not necessarily personally aware of the liminality of their social location.
For a Galilean to be personally and thus self-consciously liminal, he or
she had to appropriate it, that is, make it his or her own self-conscious
reality. Many Galileans, including Jesus, probably were at least vaguely
aware of their liminal and marginalized situation. But they may not
have automatically attained a sharp and clear consciousness of their
social predicament, or may have simply ignored the situation and lived
without paying it much attention. My suggestion, therefore, is that

Jesus left home in order to appropriate the Galilean liminality as his own personal reality. Leaving home for Jesus was an act of owning his Galilean liminality. It was a drastic act of leaving structure and an act of accepting a sharp personal awareness of his Galilean liminality.

In a recent study on Jesus and the kingdom of God, Norwegian biblical scholar Halvor Moxnes uses Victor Turner's concept of the three stages of social process (separation, liminality, reincorporation) in his analysis of the formation of the earliest Christian groups. When Jesus called his disciples, according to Moxnes, Jesus asked them to leave their household without immediately promising them a new place into which they could be reincorporated. The earliest traditions about Jesus (Q, *Gospel of Thomas*, and Mark), Moxnes points out, have Jesus calling his disciples to separate themselves from their households without entering a new household, thus leaving them dangling in a liminal space. Moxnes describes this liminal space entered by Jesus and his disciples as "a location that is not yet defined," "no-place," an "in-between position," a space of the "dislocation of identity," and a "zone of possibilities."[4]

Mark's later reinterpretation of the material in a narrative form does show that Jesus offered his displaced disciples and other followers a new and radically different household, as a representation of the reign of God. I shall return to the topic of this new household with God alone as the Father. Moxnes's point that is important here is this: according to the earliest traditions about Jesus, he left home and entered into a liminal space before he began speaking about a new household for himself and for his followers. Jesus also expected his followers to experience this stage of liminality before an alternative place of belonging was presented to them. Jesus made this demand rather sharply: "Whoever loves father or mother more than me is not worthy of me; and whoever loves son or daughter more than me is not worthy of me" (Matt. 10:37).

The episode of Jesus' rejection in his hometown confirms his new location in no-man's land. As Jesus tried to teach in the synagogue in

Nazareth, the people of the town "took offense at him." They took offense because Jesus had left "his place" in his household and in his town. He had gone beyond and out of the limits of his proper place. The town was no longer obligated to confer upon Jesus the honor that a community or social structure would bestow upon its members. He was no longer acceptable within this place. Jesus simply says, "Prophets are not without honor, except in their hometown, and among their own kin, and in their own house" (Mark 6:1-6). Jesus does not contest the town's scorn. As Moxnes puts it, "he had broken out of the mold and will not be limited by the place defined by his lineage and household. He opts to stay out of it."[5]

As discussed earlier, Galileans were living in a liminal situation because of their geographical location, political predicament, cultural diversity, and religiously peripheral situation vis-à-vis Jerusalem. Galileans were also marginalized and oppressed socioeconomically, religiously, and in other ways. Galileans' personal awareness of their objective reality of liminality and marginality would have varied in degrees depending on their individual circumstances. Jesus' perspective was that those who would respond positively to the radical new reality of the reign of God had to become personally aware of their liminality by leaving the comforts of their households. Jesus demanded that his disciples become self-consciously liminal although they already were objectively in a liminal predicament.

As we noted earlier, Galileans certainly must have been at least vaguely self-conscious of their liminality because of their objective situation. Galileans' vague but real awareness of their liminal situation may indeed be one factor behind the male disciples' willingness to make such a quick and radical departure from their homes. Simon Peter, James, and John, when called by Jesus, "brought their boats to shore, . . . left everything, and followed him" (Luke 5:11). Levi the tax collector, when called by Jesus, "got up, left everything, and followed him" (Luke 5:28). Their liminal situation had already made them open and free enough to respond quickly to Jesus. Their departure from their households undoubtedly made them even more acutely aware of their liminality than they might have been before. Such a radical liminality, a freedom from the existing structure of society, is what Jesus adopted as his own situation and demanded that his followers do likewise.

Now, why did Jesus not call women to discipleship the way he called some men, although the scriptural witness points to many women who followed him, some more closely than others? The situation must have been different for Galilean women. Perhaps the answer is that women in Galilee in general were more acutely liminal and certainly more painfully marginalized than men, by Galilee's own patriarchal culture as well as outside forces, and that many Galilean women were already subjectively conscious of their liminal and marginalized predicament. Therefore, they may not have had to leave their household as men did to become acutely conscious of their liminal and marginalized situation.[6]

Women who were closest to Jesus were indeed those who were more acutely liminal and marginalized than most Galilean women. Mary Magdalene was a single woman without any settled abode and of an ill repute. Mary and Martha in Bethany were unmarried women living with a brother. Ross Kraemer points out that "few women in the early Jesus movement appear to conform to the most socially acceptable categories of virgin daughter, respectable wife, and mother of legitimate children"[7] They were not child-bearing women. Some are said to have been widows. As Moxnes puts it, "the women we glimpse in the gospel narratives appear to be prototypes of the 'irregular' women . . . in nontraditional roles, and therefore already in marginal positions."[8] I would add that these women were not only "already marginal" but also acutely aware of their liminal and marginal status in society. It would not have made much sense for Jesus to demand that these women leave their households in order to attain a personal awareness of their liminal and marginal predicament. When Jesus met his women followers, they probably already had left their usual household structure to follow him.

The women followers of Jesus were at the forefront of all of Jesus' followers in their awareness of their social location.

JESUS' EXERCISE OF THE CREATIVE POTENTIALS OF HIS LIMINALITY

Jesus' Openness to the Father's Will

To be liminal is to be out of the structure in which a person usually functions, and, therefore, to be freed at least temporarily from what governs a person's thought and action. To be liminal is to be open to new ideas and new ways of doing things either individually or as a society. It is to be more ready than usual to consider new and different possibilities.

The openness of Jesus' liminality was a God-centered openness. Jesus in every way, including his openness, was governed and shaped by the reign of God and what God is doing through that reign. Thus, his openness was primarily openness to the will of his Father. This God-ward direction of his openness saves it from chaos. But this direction does not make his openness narrow; rather, it makes it radical. Jesus' openness is not restricted by anything other than God's will. Jesus' liminality, then, means his radical freedom from any and all creaturely principles.

Jesus' openness to God gave his liminality content. The God to whom he is absolutely loyal and open is the God whose nature is forgiving love, unlimited compassion, and graceful justice. Jesus, therefore, was steadfastly open to whatever is forgivingly loving, unlimitedly compassionate, and gracefully just.

Jesus' absolute openness to God's will is clearly discernible in his relation to the Father as witnessed to in the Gospels. Whether or not he could bring about a "miracle" of healing, and whether or not someone was going to have faith in him or not, Jesus believed was up to the Father's will and not his own. When a centurion in Capernaum showed a great faith, Jesus was "amazed" (Matt. 8:10). When Jesus was in Nazareth and found himself unable to do any "deed of power" except in a few cases, he was "amazed at their unbelief" (Mark 6:5-6). To be amazed by something is to be open to what is beyond one's own control.

Jesus' openness to his Father brought him the most agonizing moment of his life. In the garden of Gethsemane, Jesus prayed, "yet, not my will but yours be done" (Luke 22:42). Jesus was open to his Father's will to the point of death.

As we noted above, Jesus' openness to his Father also meant his freedom from anything other than his Father's will. Jesus shows this freedom in his unhesitating willingness to cross all human-made boundaries and barriers to embody his Father's forgiving love to fallen creation. To speak in anthropological language, Jesus' liminality freed him from all human-made structures and roles. He was free to move beyond the existing social and religious structures, rules, and restrictions.

Jesus crossed the boundaries of the purity code set by the religious establishment. He did not hesitate to stay overnight in chief tax collector Zacchaeus's house in order to "seek out and to save the lost" (Luke 19:10). By crossing the border and leaving behind the purity-code structure, Jesus was able to communicate to Zacchaeus God's forgiving love and unlimited compassion. Jesus let Mary, Martha's sister, sit and discuss theology with him, something that women were not allowed to do (Luke 10:39). Jesus crossed the boundaries between different peoples when he spoke to the Syro-Phoenician woman, a Gentile, and when he had a lengthy theological discussion with the Samaritan woman at the well (Mark 7:24-27; John 4:7-30). Jesus angered the Pharisees by allowing his disciples to pluck heads of grain and by healing a man with a withered hand on the Sabbath. In his answer to the Pharisees, Jesus relativized their Sabbath laws by asking them, "Is it lawful to do good or to do harm on the sabbath, to save life or to kill?" (Mark 2:23-28; 3:1-6). When the Pharisees again complained to Jesus that his disciples violated the "tradition of the elders" by eating with defiled or unwashed hands, Jesus pointed out to them there is something more ultimate than their laws about proper eating, something which would make them free from those laws. Jesus said, "You abandon the commandment of God and hold to human tradition" (Mark 7:1-8). Thus, Jesus' freedom was a freedom from everything other than the loving God and a freedom for the sake of the loving God.

Jesus' Liminality and the Emergence of *Communitas*

The second creative potential of liminality is its power to generate *communitas*. Before discussing Jesus' exercise of this potential on the basis of the Gospel records, a review of what *communitas* means is in order. *Communitas*, according to Victor Turner, can emerge between two or more persons when they are in a liminal situation—that is, freed from social norms, social roles, and hierarchy. Liminality is "the dimension . . . in which men [*sic*] confront one another not as role players but as 'human totals,' integrated beings who recognizantly share the same humanity." *Communitas* is the response to "the desire for a total, unmediated relationship between person and person," and is an "expression of men [sic] in their wholeness wholly attending."[9] *Communitas* is an egalitarian and intimate communion between two or more human beings who completely respect and accept each other in all their otherness. I take what Turner says about *communitas* as being quite close to what is generally meant by "communion" or even "loving communion" and use these terms interchangeably.

Jesus' communitas *with individuals.* The "atmosphere" of Jesus' encounter with other liminal persons in the Gospels certainly indicates the relationality of *communitas*. Since *communitas* involves two or more persons, Jesus' exercise of his liminal creativity in *communitas* naturally involves the liminality of both Jesus and the persons who experienced *communitas* with Jesus.

A good example of Jesus' *communitas* with single individuals is his encounter with Zacchaeus, a chief tax collector, mentioned earlier.

Zacchaeus's profession placed him between the Roman Empire and the Jerusalem authorities, on the one hand, and the marginalized Galilean peasants, on the other. His social location was liminality and marginalization. Jesus called him by his name and stayed at his home, ignoring the jeers by the crowd. Jesus seemed to be totally at ease with this socially ostracized person. Zacchaeus, for his part, exercised his own liminality and was thereby free enough to climb a tree to see Jesus and respond promptly to Jesus' self-invitation to his home. The whole episode exudes an atmosphere of mutual acceptance and being at ease with each other.

By crossing all human boundaries, Jesus met Zacchaeus in their mutual liminality, and experienced *communitas*. To be more accurate, Zacchaeus experienced a loving communion with God in Jesus. In and through this loving communion with God in Jesus, Zacchaeus experienced an unconditional acceptance and forgiveness by that God and became a new man.

Without the work of the Holy Spirit in both Jesus and Zacchaeus, this transformation would not have occurred. But liminal space between Zacchaeus and Jesus was a means of grace. Liminal space was a necessary but not sufficient condition for Zacchaeus's life-changing experience of *communitas* with Jesus. So *communitas* between Jesus and Zacchaeus was more than an ordinary *communitas*. It was a redemptive *communitas* in which God's infinite love was expressed. It was a redemptive communion in which Zacchaeus experienced acceptance by God, the Creator and Lord of universe.

A word is necessary here in regard to the Holy Spirit before continuing. The Holy Spirit, as noted earlier, is the eternal communion of love that emerged out of the liminality between the Father and the Son within the Trinity. In this way, the divine love, which is the essence of God, "became" the eternal *communion* between the Father and the Son, namely the Holy Spirit. The emergence of *communitas* from the liminality between Jesus and Zacchaeus is a temporal repetition of the eternal emergence of the Holy Spirit within the Trinity. In this way, the believers are taken into the communion between the Father and the Son. As the temporal repetition of the third person of the Trinity, the communion of love that emerges from the liminality between Jesus and believers is the power that will build the redeemed community on earth and is the constitutive reality of the redeemed community itself. In this way, God's infinite love, the essence of God's own being, is repeated in the temporal communion of the saints.

Jesus' communitas with his followers as a group. The category of the "followers" of Jesus is a difficult concept to define. John P. Meier arranges the overlapping clusters of followers into three concentric circles: (1) the outer circle of the crowds that followed Jesus in a physical sense (with a varying degrees of sympathetic attitudes); (2) the middle circle of "disciples" or adherents who followed Jesus in a spiritual and physical sense; and (3) the inner circle of the twelve, chosen by Jesus to symbolize his mission to the twelve tribes of Israel. Associated with the middle group are also those who remained at home and supported Jesus.[10]

The twelve were with him, as well as some women who had been cured of evil spirits and infirmities: Mary, called Magdalene, from whom seven demons had gone out; Joanna, the wife of Herod's steward, Chuza; and many others who provided for them out of their resources (Luke 8:1-3). Mark records that at the time of Jesus' crucifixion "There were also women looking on from a distance; among them were Mary Magdalene, Mary the mother of James the younger and of Joses, and Salome." Then, Mark adds, "These used to follow him and provided for him when he was in Galilee; and there were many other women who had come up with him to Jerusalem" (Mark 15:40-41).

Many women traveled with Jesus and the other men, apparently had meals together, and in other ways acted as a group. In a society where women were viewed as inferior to men and did not openly mix with men, the gender-integrated nature of Jesus' followers was unusual, to say the least. The men and women followers I am focusing on here are the inner circle of twelve, the middle group, and some of the third circle, the crowds. All these groups of Jesus' followers had one thing in common, in addition to their interest in Jesus. They were all "displaced persons," out of the ordinary structure of society. The twelve were all relatively young men who had left their households and everything they had. The middle group primarily consisted of marginalized and thus liminal persons: the sick, "sinners," and tax collectors. Those among the crowd who physically followed Jesus for a short or longer time were also most likely poor peasants who were both liminal and marginalized. Their encounter with Jesus in their common liminal space must have given rise to *communitas* among them.

Communitas *and Jesus' table-fellowship*. Nowhere is the role of liminality in generating *communitas* more clearly evident than in Jesus' act of joining for meals with socially disreputable and marginalized persons. The Pharisees asked Jesus' disciples, "Why does your teacher eat with tax collectors and sinners?" (Matt. 9:11). This practice of Jesus earned him the name "a glutton and a drunkard, a friend of tax collectors and sinners" (Matt. 11:19). This accusation, which probably came from the Pharisees, is aimed at Jesus' willingness to transgress the purity codes that prohibited Jews from socializing with impure persons, such as sinners, the sick, and tax collectors.

Eating is an activity in which people open their mouths and acknowledge their finitude (that is, dependence upon food and water) and thus an activity that exposes their vulnerability. For this reason, when people eat, they generally want to be with friends with whom they feel totally accepted and comfortable. Those who joined Jesus at meals undoubtedly felt totally accepted by him.

Jesus' compassion and love for liminal and marginalized persons moved him to be together with liminal and marginalized persons. Jesus' own liminality and the liminality of the marginalized persons whom he befriended brought them together in their common liminality. And this shared liminality was the means through which God's loving *communitas* with human beings was made possible.

Communitas, *the new family, and the reign of God*. Recall that the actual experience of *communitas*, according to Turner, is "immediate" and "spontaneous" and, therefore, transitory .

In human history, attempts have been made to preserve "spontaneous *communitas*" on a more or less permanent basis by codifying its features in a system of ethics and law. In order to preserve the original experience of *communitas*, groups would withdraw from the mainstream of a society into a voluntary separation. As Victor Turner explains, however, spontaneous *communitas* or the actual experience of *communitas* cannot be routinized or organized. But *communitas* inevitably gives way to structure.[11]

According to Turner, *communitas* and structure are in a dialectical, not antithetical, relationship. Human beings, in order to survive, must return to structure. Individuals who have experienced *communitas* can return to structure with communitarian values and can both try to practice them and also work to infuse those values into the structure. In this sense, *communitas* has a transformative function.[12]

Now if one cannot live in liminality alone, what structure did Jesus offer to his displaced and homeless followers? The structure he offered them was modeled after the most important social structure in Galilee, namely, family and household. Jesus offered them the new family of God, a family in some ways like the natural families they had left but in other respects very different from them.[13] And the new family of God for Jesus was the imperfect but proleptically real embodiment of the reign of God. In this new family the values of *communitas* that Jesus and his followers experienced together, probably again and again, were to be practiced.

The new family of God was constituted not "by birth" but "by doing the will of my Father." A crowd sitting around Jesus told him that his mother and brother were asking for him, and he responded, " 'Who are my mother and my brothers?' And looking at those who sat around him, he said, 'Here are my mother and my brothers! Whoever does the will of God is my brother and sister and mother' " (Mark 3:31-35).

This new structure is a family with brothers and sisters, but also is very different from their natural families. First of all, there is no father. Jesus said, "Call no one your father on earth, for you have one Father—the one in heaven" (Matt. 23:9). Jesus is not denying the plain fact that people have biological fathers. What he is saying is that the new family of God is not going to allow even a trace of the patriarchal subordination and dehumanization of women. Men and women are all siblings of equal dignity. Second, this new family has no hierarchy. Jesus said, referring to the status-oriented scribes and Pharisees, "They love to have the place of honor at banquets and the best seats in the synagogues, and to be greeted with respect in the marketplaces, and to have people call them rabbi." Jesus also said to his disciples and other followers:

> But you are not to be called rabbi, for you have one teacher, and you are all students. And call no one your father on earth, for you have one Father—the one in heaven. Nor are you to be called instructors, for you have one instructor, the Messiah. The greatest among you will be your servant. All who exalt themselves will be humbled, and all who humble themselves will be exalted. (Matt. 23:6-12)

The members of the new family are all students with one teacher. A question rises at this point: In Jesus' portrayal of God as "the Father," a male figure, is he not still perpetuating patriarchy? Moxnes argues that when Jesus "used the father image, it was primarily the aspect of the father who provided for his children and protected them, not the father as an authority figure." And the image of father did not necessarily encourage male supremacy in the group but, rather, put all "young men, older women, and children—into the same category as dependents in the household."[14]

Another question arises: If Jesus' followers now belong to the new family of God, does that mean that they are no longer liminal? They now have a new sense of belonging and a new identity through their participation in the new family of God. However, the reality of their liminality and marginalization as Galileans would continue. In fact, because of their new identity as members of God's family, their marginalization would become intensified, as the fleeing of male disciples from the scene of Jesus' crucifixion indicates. The experiences of liminality could also occur within the life of the new family of God, as it must have occurred at Jesus' last supper with his disciples.

Jesus' Liminality, His Prophetic Ministry, and the New Community

The third aspect of the creativity of a liminal person is his or her being at the periphery of the structure of a society and his or her ability to look at the structure with a critical perspective. Jesus used his liminal and thus critical perspective in carrying out his prophetic ministry. Jesus conducted his ministry in a context of imperial domination. The village peasants of Galilee where Jesus lived were suffering from extreme forms of economic, political, and religious oppression and exploitation at the hands of the Roman rulers and their representatives as well as the religious-economic power of the Jerusalem Temple.

A liminal, marginalized, and oppressed Galilean himself, Jesus reflected the miseries, frustrations, and protests of his fellow Galilean peasants in his actions and teachings. Jesus' ministry inevitably expressed the convictions and sentiments of the common people in response to the dominant and oppressive center.

Jesus as the incarnate Son of God, however, did not just reflect the conditions of the people. He was inaugurating the coming of the reign of God, and was building a new communion or community, a new family or household of God. In other words, Jesus' prophetic criticism of, and resistance to, the oppressive powers were meant to serve to heal and restore as well as build human community, particularly his new community as an initial realization of God's reign. Jesus' primary purpose was to actualize the purpose for which God created the world—namely, to repeat the inner-trinitarian communion in time and space. Jesus' resistance against the oppressive powers was not for resistance's sake, but for the sake of the reign of God.

Jesus' healings of the sick and crippled not only restored their physical integrity but also represented a protest against the Jerusalem Temple's purity injunctions, which had declared certain persons as "impure" and not to be touched. Moreover, Jesus' healings also restored the social relations of the sick persons. With their health restored, the healed persons could now be publicly accepted members of communities. To put it differently, the restoration of their communal life was also a part of the healing of sick persons. Bruce Malina and Richard Rohrbaugh have observed: "Illness in antiquity was a social as well as a physical phenomenon. A person with a disease or deformity was socially as well as physically abnormal. Healing therefore required re-establishing relationships as well as restoring physical health."[15]

After restoring the sight of a blind man in Bethsaida, Jesus, according to the Gospel of Mark, "sent him away to his home" (8:26). One day when a paralyzed man was brought to Jesus by his friends through the roof, Jesus first says, "Friend, your sins are forgiven you" (Luke 5:20). And then Jesus says, "'I say to you, stand up and take your bed and go to your home.' Immediately he stood up before them, took what he had been lying on, and went to his home, glorifying God" (vv. 24-25). In both cases, the cured persons are said to have gone home. Being forgiven and being physically cured deliver a person from "impurity" and restores him or her to the community. Many women "who had been cured of evil spirits and infirmities," most prominently Mary Magdalene, Joanna, and Susanna, joined the fellowship of Jesus' closest followers (Luke 8:2-3). Healing physical illnesses leads to the restoration of community.

Jesus taught his followers to protest against the oppressive powers without getting caught in the cycle of violence. Jesus' teaching in

Matthew 5:38-41 is a good example of how Jesus urged the oppressed peasants of Galilee to practice nonviolent resistance. Jesus says, "You have heard that it was said, 'An eye for an eye and a tooth for a tooth.' But I say to you, do not resist an evildoer" (vv. 38-39a). Jesus appears to forbid any kind of resistance at all. William Herzog comments, however: "Jesus was attempting to stop the spiral of violence that a violent eye-for-an-eye approach would perpetuate."[16]

Herzog's view is that although Jesus was against violence, he did not teach a passive stance in face of unjust acts. Jesus says in Matthew 5:39b, "But if any one strikes you on the right cheek, turn the other also." Herzog comments, "Assuming the assailant is right-handed, the blow was a back-handed slap, a demeaning blow delivered by a social superior to a social inferior. . . . Jesus recommended that the victim not accept the insult, but offer the other cheek, which would force the assailant to strike him with the palm of his hand, a gesture asserting his basic humanity and social standing."[17] The "eye-for-an-eye" approach would only escalate violence. To turn the other cheek offered an opportunity to break the cycle of mutual retaliation as well as a way in which one could assert one's "basic humanity as well as social standing."[18]

In verse 40, Jesus says, "And if any one wants to sue you and take your coat, give your cloak as well." Here Jesus is referring to the cruelty of a creditor and the entire system that oppresses peasant debtors. If a Jewish man gives his cloak, the second piece of his clothing, he becomes naked. By surrendering his cloak, the peasant exposes the truth of the oppressive system. This again avoids violence without being totally passive.

In verse 41, Jesus says, "And if anyone forces you to go one mile, go also the second mile." Roman soldiers had the legal permission to force people to carry something for one mile. The victim's act of going another mile would put the oppressor into a problematic situation and expose the injustice that the subjected people had to endure. Again, violence is averted but the dignity of the victim is asserted. The victim's assertion of the dignity of his or her humanity, by implication, also affirms his or her right to belong to a community.

THE DEATH OF JESUS CHRIST

Up to this point, my focus has been on the life and teaching of Jesus Christ within the framework of his exercise of the three creative potentials of his liminal social location. The events of Jesus' death and resurrection are, however, so pivotal in the Christian understanding of the meaning of Jesus Christ that I will discuss them as particular events. But these two events are not discrete. They are integrally related with, and are parts of, Jesus' life and his public ministry. His death and resurrection cannot be properly understood apart from that life and ministry.

The death of Jesus was not an accident or an isolated incident. When persons in a liminal situation exercise their liminal creativity by being single-heartedly open to the will of God, by forming an "alternative community" that challenges the status quo, and by being prophetically critical of the oppressive practices of the center, they become intolerable to the center and will inevitably be repressed or destroyed by the center. Jesus became intolerable to the religious and political authorities in Jerusalem.

Jesus did not seek his death. But he certainly risked death by living the kind of life he led, speaking and acting on behalf of the marginalized and against the unjust practices of the dominant center. Given the character of Jesus' public ministry, his death was inevitable, and he seems to have known this inevitability (Luke 17:25). Jesus embodied with single-heartedness the infinite compassion of God for the lost, the despised, and the weak. His death was an inevitable consequence of such a life. The meaning of Jesus' death, therefore, is directly connected with his life and ministry. Jesus is the Redeemer of fallen creation not just because of his death but because of the way he lived his life, which includes his death.

In his death, Jesus acted the same way he lived his life—embodying God's love and justice. As the christological hymn in Philippians puts it, "he became obedient to the point of death" (2:8). Just as he did in his ministry, Jesus on the cross was exposing, judging, and resisting the injustice of the oppressive center. And it was the power of God's love that enabled him to live the kind of life he did and also empowered him to endure the violence of the cross.

The marginalization by the dominant center that Jesus endured throughout his ministry reached its extreme point in his crucifixion. But Jesus still exercised the creative potentials of his liminality for the values of the reign of God.

Facing death, Jesus was open to his Father's will. On the cross, Jesus let his extreme liminal space generate *communitas*, and this fact needs particular attention. On the cross, Jesus' liminality reached its greatest depth. Being at the edge and "in-between" could not be more severe and poignant than it was in his death. Jesus hung in the "no-man's land" between his friends who abandoned him and his heavenly Father who he felt had forsaken him.[19] His ties with his Father who sent him and with the fallen world that he came to save were both being torn up. Only such a radical liminality, of course, could give birth to a radically new reality.

The liminal space that Jesus on the cross opens up and enters into is not an ordinary liminality for a number of important reasons:

1. First of all, Jesus' liminality on the cross is a liminality he enters in spite of the demoralizing marginalization to which he was subjected. The intention of the marginalizing forces was to marginalize Jesus to the point of death and destroy him. But Jesus had an intention of his own, and his intention was to use the liminality that accompanies marginalization for the redemption of humanity. So liminality, for Jesus, did not get suppressed and buried under the demoralizing, humiliating, and dehumanizing effects of marginalization. So Jesus opened

up and entered into his liminal space on the cross in spite of his suffering brought about by marginalization. In opening up and entering his liminal space, Jesus on the cross was resisting and indeed being victorious over the intention of the marginalizing forces that would immobilize and destroy him.

2. Jesus' liminality on the cross is an infinite liminal space because it is a liminal space that the incarnate Son of God lets himself into. The liminal space of the cross is a space that comprehends and embraces the entirety of fallen creation. In this liminality, God is not only open to but invites the totality of God's broken world.

3. Jesus' entrance into his liminal space on the cross in spite of the effects of marginalization means God's entrance into and participation in Jesus' liminality and suffering, and, through him, in the suffering of fallen creation. As Jürgen Moltmann and others have pointed out, God out of God's love for humanity participates in their suffering. Moltmann has gone so far as to say that the Son suffers the pain of being abandoned by his Father, while the Father suffers the pain of grief in losing his Son on the cross.[20] Wonhee Anne Joh has, rightly I believe, criticized Moltmann for being rather preoccupied with the trinitarian meaning of God's participation in human suffering at the cost of not paying sufficient attention to humanity's participation in the cross.[21] My own discussion of the human beings' participation in Jesus' liminality corrects the problem at least to a certain extent.

4. This liminal space is not a space in which Jesus the Son of God and some human beings enter together at the same time. This space is brought about by God's gracious love of marginalized human beings because of which God in Jesus resisted and rejected the dehumanizing structures in the world. The liminal space opened up by the cross of Jesus is brought about by God's compassion for people who offend the authorities. In

this infinite space of liminality, all the dislocation people experience, all the thresholds people are pushed to, the depth of uncertainty that finite beings experience, and the suffering of all living beings are to be comprehended.

5. The liminal space of the cross is the infinite space the loving God opens up in Jesus. Therefore, those who enter this space will not fully comprehend the meaning of the prior presence of Jesus in this space unless they understand him in connection with all the liminal spaces he opened up in the process of loving and healing marginalized human beings during his public ministry in Galilee and elsewhere. The One whom those who enter this space encounter is not just Jesus who is being killed on the cross but is the Galilean Jesus who loved Mary and Martha, Peter and Andrew, who was criticized for eating together with sinners, and who stayed in Zacchaeus's house overnight.

6. All liminal spaces generate *communitas* of the persons who are in those spaces. Those persons who enter the liminal space of Jesus and encounter him will also experience *communitas* with him and with each other. But there is much more. Those who enter Jesus' liminal space experience *communitas* with Jesus as the loving communion with the God who out of infinite grace forgives sinners and accepts his unacceptable children and as the God who grants them the ability to live a new life. The human phenomenon of the emergence of *communitas* out of liminality is used here as a means or a form in and through which something that is infinitely higher than common *communitas* is communicated. Out of the liminality of Jesus on the cross comes, by the work of the Holy Spirit, the redeeming and transforming *communitas* with God Godself.

7. The liminal space of Jesus on the cross is an invitation to all people to come in and experience the redeeming and transforming *communitas* with God in Jesus who is already in that liminal space. By opening up this liminal space out of God's

love of God's children, God has taken the initiative. But God's act of reconciling with fallen humanity is not a one-way street. Human beings must enter that space. I shall return to this point in the following chapter.

One should not fail to note that those who were the first to be with Jesus in the liminal space of the cross were "Mary Magdalene, and Mary the mother of James the younger and of Joses, and Salome, . . . [as well as] other women who had come up with him to Jerusalem" (Mark 15:40-41). These were among those who experienced *communitas* with Jesus during his pre-crucifixion and resurrection period. *Communitas* with Jesus in that period, we might say, was a prelude or foretaste of the full redeeming *communitas* they experienced with Jesus on the cross. And the resurrection of the crucified Jesus confirms the eternal validity and power of the fully redeeming *communitas* with Jesus on the cross. Present also in that liminal space with Jesus were the centurion and one of the criminals being executed next to Jesus. These persons experienced the redeeming *communitas* with God in Jesus in that liminal space, and provide a continuity between Jesus' *communitas* with his close followers during his ministry, on the one hand, and with his *communitas* after his resurrection, on the other.

THE RESURRECTION
OF THE CRUCIFIED JESUS

Jesus really died and was buried. Therefore, only God the Creator of the universe could bring Jesus back to life. The grief-stricken Father raised his beloved Son from the dead in the power of the Holy Spirit. Connecting God the Creator to the resurrection points out the truth that the raising of Jesus was the death of death, and this overcoming of death was necessary not only for the eternal life of individual believers but, more ultimately, for the accomplishment of the end for which God created the world—namely, the repetition in time and space of the beauty of the loving communion within the inner-trinitarian life.

The fact that the resurrection was the resurrection of the crucified Jesus means that the One who is raised from the dead is Jesus
the Galilean, who lived and gave his life for the embodiment of God's
forgiving love, unlimited grace, and loving justice. The power of God's
love, in other words, is the ultimately real and the ultimately powerful
reality, and death will never be the last word. The violent, demoralizing, and dehumanizing powers of the marginalizing centers of this
world are finally judged and overcome in the crucifixion and resurrection of Jesus.

The resurrection of Jesus Christ, however, did not simply endorse
Jesus' ministry prior to his death, nor is the resurrection simply the
annulment of the power of death. As Moltmann has pointed out, the
resurrection of the crucified Christ has to be seen as having an "added
value and surplus" over against the death of Jesus.[22] The resurrection
of Jesus was also an event in which Jesus became the "first fruits of
those who have died" (1 Cor. 15:20). The risen Jesus is the first fruits
of the eschatological new creation in which "God will wipe away every
tear from their eyes" (Rev. 7:17). This complete realization of the reign
of God has begun in Jesus in a decisive way. Thus, those who are united
to this risen Jesus through their faith are to begin leading a completely
new existence. Through Jesus' resurrection, the ultimate significance
of death has been cancelled. But while leading a wholly new existence,
death still remains as something that Jesus' followers have to face. The
coming of the world where death will be no more for human beings is
yet in the future. In the meantime, those who are united with Christ
live from Christ's resurrection—that is, with a hope and yearning for
the future and with an ever-increasing resistance and protest against
the powers of death and injustice that still remain in the world.

Paul says that Christ was raised "for our justification" (Rom. 4:25).
How is justification related to Jesus' resurrection? For one thing, Jesus'
resurrection confirms the forgiveness of sins brought about through
the cross of Jesus. But Jesus' resurrection does more than take away
the sting of sin which is death. Salvation by Christ is not just the

"cancellation of sin," but a new righteousness, an entirely new existence. If we were reconciled with God through Jesus' death, "much
more surely . . . will we be saved by his life" (Rom. 5:10). Justification
is not just an imputation of the remission of sins but also the reception
of "eternal life." Jesus' resurrection is not merely the restoration of the
original creation but a further increase of the repetition of God's glory
in time and space. Through Jesus' resurrection, therefore, his believers
enter an entirely new life in which they work for the final realization of
God's love and justice in this world.

The resurrection of Jesus confirms that the love of God will have
the final say in the world. But this hope should not set a Christian on
a triumphalistic path. There are still resistances to God's love and to
God's building of loving communion in time and history. And the ultimate realization of this love in all aspects of life does not appear in the
usual historical development. But still the Christian hope is in the love
of God, as Walter Kasper puts it, "a love which has made its appearance eschatologically and finally in the death and Resurrection of
Jesus; a love to which henceforth all that is future belongs, and belongs
underivably." Kasper continues, "Hope of that kind permits of no historical speculation, but certainly invites historical practice. The belief
that love persists for ever (1 Cor. 13:8) means that only that which is
done of love will endure for ever and is lastingly inscribed in the condition and growth of reality."[23]

Now, one may ask: What does Jesus' resurrection mean for his
liminality and marginalization? As noted above, Jesus' resurrection
from death confirmed that the marginalizing forces in the world are
not the ultimately real powers, and that the extreme form of marginalization, namely death, is proved to have no ultimate power over the
life-creating power of the loving and compassionate God.

For Asian American believers who have united with Jesus in his
liminality and *communitas*, however, their social liminality and marginality in the United States have not been changed by their Lord's
victory over the marginalizing forces. Their empirical, social situation

remains the same as before. But the resurrection of Jesus in another sense has changed everything. Asian Americans who are united with Jesus are now united with the resurrected Jesus, and need not be afraid to face the disorienting and bewildering experience of liminality. They also need not be demoralized by their marginalization by the dominant white society. Dehumanizing marginalization has proven to be impotent in Jesus' victory over death. Asian Americans need not be afraid to resist the evils of injustice, or to cross borders and boundaries to communicate God's forgiving love and unlimited compassion to the weak and the oppressed in society. Asian American Christians know that it is God's love that has already overcome all the marginalizing forces, including death, and that only God's love of us will endure forever.

THE EXALTATION OF JESUS CHRIST

After appearing to his disciples, the resurrected Jesus was taken up "into heaven" (Acts 1:11) to be seated "at the right hand of God" (Rom. 8:34). Jesus the Galilean who is the incarnate Son of God now entered the "dimension" of God to share in divine power (Rom. 1:3f.) and divine glory (Phil. 3:21). From this position of power, he intercedes with the Father for us (Rom. 8:34) and protects us on the day of God's judgment (Rom. 5:9). God the Father will not rule the world except through the spirit of the incarnate Son who is at God's right hand. Jesus gave all to the Father and to fallen humanity in his life and ministry. Jesus gave all to the Father and fallen humanity on the cross. In raising the crucified Jesus from the dead, God accepted all that the incarnate Son was and did. In bringing the incarnate Son to his side, God completed God's acceptance of the incarnate Son and what he did.[24]

The exalted Jesus intercedes for us with the Father. The exalted Christ also continues his earthly ministry now as the exalted Lord in the power of the Holy Spirit. He continues to move the world in the direction of accomplishing God's end in creation. With divine authority, the exalted Jesus guarantees that he himself, and not the power of death and evil, will have the final say at the end of history.

It is of utmost importance to remember the corporeal nature of the resurrection. If the historicity of the resurrection is taken seriously, then the corporeality follows from that. As an actual historical man, Jesus of Nazareth is inconceivable without his body. What Paul calls *soma pneumatikon* is the genuine body, which is entirely directed by the Spirit of God. So the whole person of the Lord is finally with God. Sitting "at the right hand of God," the exalted Christ has the divine power of judgment at the end of this world, which is the power to protect those united with him against death and judgment.

That the exalted Jesus is now in God's sphere, however, does not mean that he has no contact with the world. Precisely the corporeality of the exalted Lord means that he continues to be with the world. Now he is with God in the divine sphere; therefore, he is with the world in a divine way and that means in a totally new way. In Walter Kasper's words, "Jesus' permanent and yet new way of being for us and with us is most clearly expressed in the Eucharist, where Christ gives himself to us and communicates with us." Christ is now with us in "a new divine way."[25]

That the exalted Jesus is with us also can only mean that the community of Jesus which is still on earth has an eternal dimension; Jesus' community is tied up permanently with the exalted head of that community. The seemingly fragile community of consciously liminal and marginalized Asian American followers of Jesus has the exalted Lord as its head and leader. This tie of the Asian American church with the exalted Lord is its eschatological future and divinely guaranteed promise. And that promise is the source of Asian American believers' courage to live in awareness of their liminal space and the source of endurance in their struggle against marginalization.

Chapter 5

REDEMPTION IN ASIAN AMERICAN CONTEXT

THE MEANING OF ATONEMENT

According to Paul, "In Christ, God was reconciling the world to himself" (2 Cor. 5:19). Humanity's resistance to God's will brought about a brokenness in their relationship with God. God takes the initiative in Christ to mend this brokenness. The articulation of how this reconciliation happens is the Christian doctrine of atonement.

The church's doctrines of atonement have pointed especially to Jesus' death on the cross as the event of atonement. In recent years, however, theologians have begun to see Jesus' entire ministry—including, of course, his death on the cross and the resurrection—as God's work of reconciliation with the fallen creation. I will quickly review the traditional doctrines and point out the weaknesses of each doctrine as well as its meaningfulness, especially in the Asian American context. I will then proceed to outline my own understanding of the meaning of atonement within the context of the theological perspective thus far articulated.

The first well-known traditional atonement doctrine is the *Christus Victor* theory, which explains Jesus' redemptive work on the cross as a cosmic battle (Col. 2:15) between God and the forces of evil. Shrouded in human flesh, the Son of God fools the evil forces into thinking he is an easy prey. Christ on the cross lets the "fish" swallow him all the way so that the victory of the resurrection would be complete. Admittedly, there are numerous problems with this theory: first, the fishing imagery, when taken literally, reduces Jesus to mere prey. Second, by positing coeval forces of opposition over against God, the cosmic-battle idea engenders dualistic implications. Finally, the whole redemptive drama takes places in abstraction from fallen humanity itself—it speaks of a drama in which humans have no role whatsoever.[1]

However, the idea of Christ's complete victory over the evil forces, principalities, and powers that keep human beings in bondage to sin and marginalization is important and meaningful for those who live at the margins of society. As discussed earlier, racism is an example of cultural and social forces greater than the individuals who practice it. In their resistance to racism and struggle for justice, marginalized people can easily fall into feeling that their enemy is insurmountable and that their struggle is futile. The conviction that in Jesus Christ God has decisively defeated the evil forces and that their complete collapse will eventually follow gives marginalized people a fundamental hope without which they cannot continue to struggle against injustice.

Another influential theory of the atonement is the so-called *Anselmian satisfaction theory*. Based on the scriptural references to Christ's "vicarious suffering," this theory is typically articulated within the framework of the medieval system of law, offense, and reparations. Human beings' disobedience to God dishonors God, and either satisfaction must be given or punishment must follow. Since finite humanity cannot make up for the infinite dishonor done to God, the Son of God himself had to take humanity's place as a substitute, and Jesus suffers the punishment due to sinful humanity. In this way, the Lawgiver is satisfied and God's mercy can now be shown to sinners.

The greatest problem with this theory, as has often been pointed out, is that it seems to set up a conflict within God between divine mercy and justice.[2] Grace appears to be conditional. As Daniel Migliore has noted, this theory "draws upon the juridical metaphors of the New

Testament in a way that brings mercy and justice into collision." Karl Barth moves beyond Anselm and interprets "the atoning work of Christ as motivated solely by the holy love of God." In this way, the Anselmian emphasis upon punishment satisfying the demand of justice *quid pro quo* recedes into the background.[3]

The third influential theory of atonement is the *moral example* or the *moral influence theory*, first formulated by Abelard, a contemporary of Anselm. This theory is usually understood as one in which the exemplary power of God's love in Jesus Christ is intended to generate a response from fallen humanity that changes their lives. Abelard, in some passages of his writings, goes beyond the idea of the example of God's love and refers to God's love in Christ as a divine benefit and love that generates love in the hearts of sinful humanity. The usual criticism of this theory is that it underestimates the seriousness of the fallen condition by assuming that Jesus' example alone can liberate humanity from its bondage to sin. The theory gains strength, however, if Jesus' exemplary life is conceived of as possessing a creative power that brings about a real change in the human condition.[4] The strength of the moral influence theory, understood in this sense, has the advantage of envisaging redemption as an event that deeply involves the inner subjects of those who are being redeemed.

The Christian church has not designated any of the above theories as the orthodox doctrine of atonement. In fact, some truth about God's reconciling work in Christ may be found in each of the theories we mentioned above. The variety of understandings of atonement in the history of the church gives us the freedom to articulate our own understanding of atonement based upon the Scriptures and Asian Americans' experiences of being reconciled to God in Christ.

God's act of bringing sinful human beings back into a right relationship with God occurs in the infinite space of Christ's liminality in which sinners experience the redeeming communion with God in Jesus and the beginning of a new life. The Christ whom sinners encounter in that space is Jesus who loved people to the point of his death on the cross. Jesus' crucifixion and resurrection are pivotal points in Jesus' life and ministry, but the Jesus that sinners encounter is Jesus in his entire earthly ministry: the way he loved people, the way he suffered, and all that he taught. The point is that what saves the sinner is the gracious God's unconditional love as embodied in Jesus in the entirety of his life and ministry. Jesus embodied God's unconditional love of people "to the point of death—even death on a cross" (Phil. 2:8).

Between the believers and Christ in the infinite space of liminality of Jesus, the redeeming *communitas* emerges in the power of the Holy Spirit. In this redeeming *communitas*, believers experience the unconditional acceptance by God and a transformation for a new life. In that communion, believers become united with Jesus and with all others who are already united with him.

Jesus' suffering and death on the cross has a particular significance in God's redemptive work in Jesus in that his suffering and death make the way he lived all his life authentic and life-changing. But it is not Jesus' suffering on the cross as such or his death on the cross as such that is redemptive and reconciling. As Wonhee Anne Joh puts it, "What is significant about the cross, then, is not that Jesus died on it but that because of his living out of *jeung* [love], he ended up de facto on the cross."[5]

God's forgiveness of sinners was not granted *quid pro quo* in return for Jesus' death on the cross. If we say that it was Jesus' death as such that made God's forgiveness possible, we would be promoting violence and punishment and making God's grace conditional. What saves sinners is God's sovereign grace.

Jesus' death on the cross, however, has a particular significance. Jesus' suffering to the point of death makes it a testimony to the costly and serious nature of God's love and forgiveness, and enables the communication of God's love to forgiven sinners. Daniel Day Williams argues in his book *The Nature and Forms of Love* that the love of a lover which does not involve the lover's self-giving and suffering cannot touch the heart of the one who is loved.[6] Only a costly act of forgiveness can heal the guilty. The fact that Jesus' love of the people was "to the point of death" authenticates that love. Jesus' suffering and death do not pay for God's forgiveness of the sinner, but make that forgiveness authentic and effectual.

Jesus said, "No one has greater love than this, to lay down one's life for one's friends" (John 15:13). To lay down one's life because of love demonstrates that such love is "greater" than any other kind of love. God has shown God's love for and forgiveness of sinful humanity to the utmost point possible. So Paul's statement that "we were reconciled to God through the death of his Son" (Rom. 5:10) is to be understood in light of his other statement two verses before that "God proves his love for us in that while we still were sinners Christ died for us" (v. 8). So God's work of reconciling fallen humanity to Godself and to each other consists in God's costly embrace of humanity with God's unconditional love and forgiveness and thereby making a new life possible for forgiven sinners.

In addition to authenticating God's love, there is yet another way in which Jesus' suffering and death on the cross are significant for the redemption of fallen humanity. Jesus stands in the place of human beings to take upon himself the consequences of God's wrath toward the sin of humanity. God cannot condone or overlook the sinfulness of human beings although God loves them. God's wrath toward human sinfulness must be expressed. But human beings cannot bear the brunt of God's anger and still live. So Jesus Christ puts himself in the place of human beings and accepts God's punishment on behalf of fallen humanity. It is important to note here that Jesus does not take God's punishment in order to make *quid pro quo* God's expression of God's mercifulness possible. Jesus' suffering and death on the cross does not purchase human redemption. Rather, the cross is the expression of God's love of sinful humanity. Out of God's mercifulness toward humanity, God took the punishment Godself. So "Christ died for our sins in accordance with the scriptures" (1 Cor. 15:3). "But he was wounded for our transgressions, crushed for our iniquities . . . and the Lord has laid on him the iniquity of us all" (Isaiah 53:5, 6).

In the context of marginalized Asian Americans, we need to interpret God's costly love in Christ also as an act of healing the wounds. Andrew Sung Park maintains that traditional Western theology has defined redemption primarily as the forgiveness of sins and has neglected the need for healing the oppressed peoples. Park goes further and asserts that "sin is of oppressors; *han* ['the collapsed anguish of the heart' due to unjust oppression] is of the oppressed."[7]

I may not agree with Park on his sharp distinction between the oppressors (sinners) and the oppressed as victims. However, his assertion that Asian American theology must consider healing the wounds as an essential dimension of God's redemptive work is an important contribution. Learning from Park, then, we must emphasize that God's redemptive work through the *communitas* of Jesus is not only an experience of forgiveness and acceptance by God's grace but also an experience of healing. Marginalized Asian Americans need the healing of their demoralized selves so that with renewed self-esteem and courage they may be empowered to exercise the creative potentials of their liminality which have been suppressed and frustrated.

Wendy Farley, in her *Tragic Vision and Divine Compassion: A Contemporary Theodicy*, offers a helpful discussion of the healing power of divine compassion. "Compassion is love as it encounters suffering," says Farley.[8] She also explains that because compassion is love, it is able to see through the wounds of the sufferer and recognize the goodness of the sufferer's personhood. In this way, compassion communicates "respect" to the sufferer and considers what has happened to the sufferer as "alien" to the sufferer's personhood.

Farley goes on to explain the healing work of compassion:

[Compassion] begins where the sufferer is, in the grief, the shame, the hopelessness. It sees the despair as the most real thing. Compassion is with the sufferer, turned toward or submerged in her experience, seeing it with her eyes. The communion with the sufferer in her pain, as she experiences it, is the presence of love that is a balm to the wounded spirit. This relationship of shared, sympathetic suffering mediates consolation and respect that empower the sufferer to bear the pain, to resist the humiliation, and to overcome the guilt.[9]

Compassion leads to a "communion with the sufferer in pain." Such a caring communion does not merely "comfort" the sufferer but also "empowers" the spirit of the wounded. "Compassion labors to penetrate the darkness of pain and mediate to the sufferer the taste of love and the power of courage."[10] Compassion does something to the basic orientation of the wounded self and enables him or her to be and to act in a new way.

Rita Nakashima Brock interprets God's power of healing as the power that works through the "erotic power" of the heart. And the "erotic power" of the heart," according to Brock, is "the power of our primal interrelatedness." For Brock, it is "the divine erotic power [that] liberates, heals, and makes whole through our willingness to participate in mutuality."[11] God's power of love, according to Brock, heals the "brokenheartedness" of oppressed people through the concrete and actual "connectedness" that the community of Christ makes possible. In other words, the *communitas* of Jesus is the redemptive and healing experience only as a person participates in that *communitas* as a concrete connectednessness. I shall return to this point below.

Instructive also for our own understanding of the healing is Wonhee Anne Joh's interpretation of God's love as *jeung*, a concept she appropriates from Korean culture and life. *Jeung*, she says, means love, but is more "expansive and generous than love."[12] Between *jeung* and *communitas*, there seems to be a great deal of continuity, although the notion of *communitas* can also be enriched by Joh's interpretation of *jeung*. *Jeung*, says Joh, "encompasses but is not limited to the notions of compassion, affection, solidarity, vulnerability, and forgiveness." *Jeung* knows no boundaries or borders. *Jeung* even sees beyond the dichotomy set up between the oppressors and the oppressed. *Jeung* can even "recognize the brokenness and pain of the oppressors because of the fear that drives them to commit violence and mete out death toward others."[13] Joh also asserts that "*jeung* is the divine presence that nudges us not only to perceive but also accept the often negativized and shadowed parts of ourselves and thus ultimately to awaken to and practice the way of living in the fullness of *jeung*."[14] Like *jeung*, the experience of the *communitas* of Christ needs to be understood as an experience in which the oppressor–the oppressed dichotomy is transcended.

The way in which Joh relates *jeung* to liminality is also instructive. According to Joh, *jeung* "resides in" and "comes forth" within the "interstitial spaces," "within the gaps and fissures," and the "in-between spaces." *Jeung* arises, in other words, in liminal spaces. But, for Joh, *jeung* also "creates" and "opens up" liminal spaces.[15] *Jeung* and liminal spaces are in a two-way relationship. *Communitas*, in my view, is an egalitarian relationality that challenges the way societies are usually organized. One can easily see how a person with an experience of *communitas* could return to the usual social structure and "open up" gaps or liminal spaces in the usual ways of people's thinking. Healing brings "wholeness" both in the sense of empowerment and also in the sense of becoming open to new ideas and realities.

So healing is an essential aspect of redemption and is not merely a symptomatic relief of the hurt of marginalized persons. Healing in Asian American theology has to do with the transformation in the way human beings are and act. Healing means to become "healers," to have one's "image of God" restored (Park), to become a "whole and compassionate being" (Brock), and to be a self without excluding others (even the oppressors) (Joh).[16] Healing, in short, is an essential aspect of becoming a "new creation," and, therefore, an essential aspect of the redemption of Asian Americans as a marginalized people.

BELIEVERS' RESPONSE TO AND PARTICIPATION IN ATONEMENT

Thus far in this chapter, I have outlined an understanding of redemption as the experience of God's unconditional love in and through a participation in the redeeming *communitas* that emerges in and through the liminal space of Jesus. In this experience, sinners experience forgiveness and are empowered to live a new life exercising the creative potentials of liminality in spite of the reality of continuing marginalization. Jesus' suffering in his life, ministry, and on the cross is the consequence of Jesus' risk taking and boundary crossing in his steadfast embodiment of God's love of people. Jesus' suffering and death make God's love in Jesus authentic and effectual. Finally, I have argued that in the context of marginalized people, such as Asian Americans, healing is an essential aspect of being redeemed.

It must now be stressed that atonement, as I am articulating it here, is a process in which the human response is an essential part. The initiative in atonement is God's grace. There is absolutely nothing that human beings can do to make atonement possible. And yet atonement involves human participation. Atonement is not something that happens apart from human beings. Atonement is actualized in and through communion between Christ and sinners. Human beings must enter into the liminal space of Jesus and be with him if there is going to be any redeeming communion between them.

Before a person enters Jesus' liminal space to unite with him, that person must first have a perception of Jesus in all of his concreteness: his deeds, his words, his way with other persons, his death, and his resurrection. This perception, of course, is not an impersonal and detached knowledge but a knowing in which one is attracted, grasped, and moved by the figure of Jesus. One must then move into Jesus' liminal space and meet him in that space. Such an act of "closing with" Christ in his liminal space, to borrow an expression from Jonathan Edwards, can happen as one participates in the liminality of worship or the Lord's Supper in which Christ is the center of attention.[17] One could also unite with Christ in an ordinary experience of liminality if the image of Christ is the center of attention. Liminality is the space in which one is freed from social and cultural structure and status. Being in a liminal space today can overlap and coalesce with the experience of being in Jesus' space of infinite liminality. Or, to put it differently, our concrete experience of liminal space with Christ as the center of attention mediates for us now (connects us to) the liminal space that Jesus entered two thousand years ago.

In that liminal space of Jesus, a redeeming *communitas* can occur between God in Jesus and us, fallen but believing human beings. What is generated in that liminal space, in the power of the Holy Spirit working in believing human beings and through the dynamics of liminal creativity, is an experience of being unconditionally accepted and forgiven by God in Christ, who is the author of our life and the entire system of being and in whose hands ultimately lies the meaning of life itself. *Communitas* functions as that in and through which an unbelievable communion with the forgiving and loving God comes alive in and for the believing sinner.

The faith response of the believer, then, is one action of the believing sinner but has two moments: (1) entering into Christ's liminal space and (2) embracing or accepting God's love in Christ in the experience of Jesus' *communitas*. Jonathan Edwards also speaks of the two "moments" in the one response of faith. In a notebook on "Faith," Edwards tries out many definitions of faith. One of those definitions reads: "Faith consists in two things, viz. in being persuaded of and embracing the promises (Heb. 11:13)."[18] If one were not aware of, and, to some extent, attracted by the character and life of Jesus, that person would not take the step of entering Jesus' liminal space. At the same time, it is in *communitas* with Jesus that a person experiences fully the unconditional acceptance of God in Jesus and accepts and embraces God's acceptance. Perhaps the two aspects of faith we are speaking about here are in a continuum. The first act of entering Jesus' liminal space is the initial or preliminary act of moving toward Christ with a sense of the attractiveness of Christ and his life. And the second phase is the proper and fuller experience of being loved by God and one's accepting response to that love. Perhaps, just as Edwards, we cannot arrive at a completely satisfactory analysis of the human response called "faith," which is a gift of the Holy Spirit.

The implication of this is the truth that, for those human beings who live today and did not have a direct encounter with Jesus, the redemptive experience of Jesus in his liminal space has to be mediated. There are two related but distinguishable mediations here. First, the figure of Jesus the Galilean has to be communicated to persons who live two thousand years after the time of Jesus. The Word has to be meditated, in other words. The gospel of Jesus to which the Scriptures bear witness has to be communicated. The church's task, therefore, is to proclaim the good news embodied in Jesus' life both in word and in deed. Sermons, worship, educational programs, and other appropriate vehicles must communicate to people today what Jesus was all about.

But the proclamation by itself would not be sufficient. Many people know a great deal about who Jesus was and what he did, but are not transformed by it. This is the point where the Holy Spirit's work of inspiring the hearer of Jesus' gospel is crucial. The Holy Spirit works in and through the natural functions of the human mind, affections, and the imagination and leads a person to see God's presence in who Jesus was and what Jesus did. This perception of God in Jesus is not something human beings can bring about or acquire through human means. The Holy Spirit, on the other hand, does not work in the darkness. The Holy Spirit works with the Word that has been proclaimed to people today. The Word and the Spirit can never be separated. And the Word and Spirit work in and through the natural functions of human beings.

I said above that what mediates Jesus Christ to people today is the church's proclamation of the gospel of Jesus Christ in word and deed. Persons living today do not have a concrete encounter of Jesus in a direct fashion. And without a concrete experience of the unconditional love embodied in Jesus, persons today would only have an abstract idea about that love. When someone says, "Jesus loves you and so do we," Jesus' love is abstract and does not really touch the heart and mind of someone who is alive today. This is the reason why members of the church must exemplify Jesus' kind of love to other persons. When a church member does embody an unconditional love to someone, that love is concrete and will touch someone's heart. Such a human embodiment of unconditional love will make Christ's own love come alive to the beloved person. The mediating Word, therefore, is both in word and in deed. The Holy Spirit, working in and through the natural functions of a human being, enables him or her to experience Christ's unconditional love. The Holy Spirit also enables the person to see God's unconditional love and forgiveness in Christ. But the Holy Spirit does this in conjunction with the Christ who has been made concrete today by someone who embodies such love to another person.

Søren Kierkegaard, a nineteenth-century philosopher-theologian, insisted that those persons who were contemporaries of Jesus did not have any advantage over those living today.[19] His point was that whether one actually encountered Jesus in person or hears about him today, it would require the same inspiration of the Holy Spirit if he or she is going to make a faith response to God in Jesus. Kierkegaard was emphasizing the all-important response of faith by the believer and the inspiration of the Holy Spirit in that faith. In this emphasis upon the subjective response to Christ, Kierkegaard downplayed the role of the concrete history of Jesus that elicits the faith response. Thus, the concrete details of Jesus' life, death, and resurrection would have to be in the front of our minds if the Holy Spirit is going to work through a person and bring about that person's faith response and his or her experience of redeeming *communitas* with Jesus.

JUSTIFICATION OF THE MARGINALIZED

The purpose of God's redemptive work in Jesus Christ is the transformation of the fallen world into a new creation. The first moment in sinful humanity's new existence in Christ is the justification by grace through faith. The justification of "the ungodly" is completely an unmerited act of God's grace and means the forgiveness of sinners and the restoration of their relationship with God.

The Pauline doctrine that sinners are accepted as righteous through the imputation of Christ's righteousness and not by the sinners' adherence to the law constitutes a fundamental rejection of human achievement as the ground of salvation. The doctrine of justification therefore relativizes all finite principles as the ultimate source of the worth of human persons before God. Neither condemnation by the law nor disparagement by any finite power can be the cause of a person's ultimate loss of his/her worth as a person. As Paul declares, "For I am convinced that neither death, nor life, nor angels, nor rulers, nor things present, nor things to come, nor powers, nor height, nor depth, nor anything else in all creation, will be able to separate us from the love of God in Christ Jesus our Lord" (Rom. 8:38-39).

Justification by God's grace gives a person an identity and a sense of dignity that cannot be shaken and is, therefore, good news for Asian Americans. The doctrine of justification says that Asian Americans are God's children even when they are invisible to white American society. Justification doctrine says God accepts Asian Americans when white Americans judge them as "not American enough," and Asians in Asia judge them "not Asian enough." Justification says that Asian Americans belong to God and to the family of God when they feel as if they do not belong either to America or to Asia.

In the marginalized Asian Americans' context, justification means acceptance, belonging, recognition, and inclusion. The author of 1 Peter expresses well the meaning of justification for people who are treated as strangers by the society in which they live. Writing to

Christian Jews living in Asia Minor, the epistle's author says, "But you are a chosen race, a royal priesthood, a holy nation, God's own people. . . . Once you were not a people, but now you are God's people; once you had not received mercy, but now you have received mercy" (1 Pet. 2:9-10).

The objective reality of God's act of justifying the sinner through God's grace, however, becomes a personal reality only through the sinner's act of faith. If the sinner's life as a "new creation" is going to be realized, the sinner's act of faith must be followed up by the process of sanctification. In other words, justification and sanctification are inseparable. The salvation of the sinner does not mean only being forgiven; it is also a real change in the sinner's life.

Both justification of sinners without any merit of their own and a real change in their actual lives have the same foundation: namely communion with the loving God in Christ. There can be no justification without sanctification and there can be no sanctification without justification. The one-sided emphasis upon justification as forgiveness and imputed righteousness leads to a neglect of the real change in the sinner's life. An emphasis on forgiveness without equal attention to sanctification leads to an individualization of salvation and to an apolitical piety. A marginalized person can revel in the euphoria of his or her personal salvation and totally neglect his or her responsibilities for other persons and the world. Jesus did not just want to forgive people; he also wanted to restore the marginalized people's physical health, social well-being, and political justice. Jesus healed the sick and in doing so restored their standing in the community. Jesus stood up against the Roman Empire and the Jerusalem Temple, both of which oppressed people. For marginalized people such as Asian Americans their justification before God, therefore, has to be accompanied by a new direction in all aspects of their lives.

Andrew Sung Park, as noted above, has sharply challenged the traditional formulation of the doctrine of justification by faith. Park insists that the needs of the oppressors (the sinners) and the oppressed (the "sinned against") are different. Sinners need mercy and forgiveness, while the sinned against need justice and vindication. Park refers to Old Testament writings such as Habakkuk where faith means to "wait for God's judgment upon the wicked." Park writes, "Trusting in the faithfulness of God for the restoration of justice is the gist of Habakkuk's faith. . . . Since the church has treated the faith of the sinners, it needs to balance the view by lifting up the faith of the sinned against in the Bible."[20] For Park the faith of the oppressors (sinners) is in justification and forgiveness, while the faith of the sinned against is a faith in God's vindication of the oppressed through the establishment of justice. Justice, according to Park, will lead to the healing of the wounds of the sinned against.

Park's point that justification for the oppressed must include the establishment of justice and the healing of their wounds is an important contribution to Asian American theology. But one wonders whether Park's sharp separation between justification for sinners and justice for the sinned against is really necessary. For one thing, all have sinned, both the oppressors and the oppressed (Rom. 3:22). Sin includes more than oppression. Sin is also self-centeredness, pride, and idolatry. Justification in the sense of God's acceptance of sinners solely by God's grace is for both the oppressors and the oppressed.

Second, justification is unthinkable without the establishment of justice and the healing of the wounded. The principle of the inseparability of justification from sanctification would seem to include Park's legitimate concern that redemption for the oppressed is meaningless without the establishment of justice and the healing of the wounds.

Andrew Park's emphasis that justification for the oppressed must mean justice and healing is a valuable reminder that the justification-by-grace-alone doctrine has sometimes been abused and misunderstood in such a way that the practice of justice is ignored. As I mentioned above, however, justification doctrine has sometimes been abused as the basis of a do-nothing complacency and also of a one-sidedly individualistic faith.

The justification doctrine, rightly understood, as Harold Wells explains, has "the power to undermine the moral smugness and superiority that feed so much human hatred and conflict." Wells points out further that "the doctrine of justification is a reconciling doctrine if both victims and their perpetrators cease to claim a righteousness of their own and acknowledge their own need for forgiveness and grace."[21]

REPENTANCE

One of John Calvin's creative insights is that repentance follows faith instead of preceding it. Calvin writes, "Repentance not only constantly follows faith, but is born of faith." Calvin explains further, "A man [*sic*] cannot apply himself seriously to repentance without knowing himself [*sic*] to belong to God. But no one is truly persuaded that he belongs to God unless he has first recognized God's grace."[22] Calvin's point is that only when sinners know how deeply God loves them and therefore values them do they truly realize how serious a matter their rebellion against and distrust in God was.

According to Calvin, faith is followed not only by repentance or turning away from one's sinful self but also by a new life in Christ or turning toward God. Calvin calls these two aspects of repentance "mortification and vivification." So, for Calvin, repentance in its broad sense means both turning away from sin and also beginning a new life by turning to God. "If we are truly partakers in his [Christ's] death," wrote Calvin, "by virtue of this our old man is crucified, and the mass of sin remaining in us is mortified. . . . When we participate in his resurrection, we are thereby revivified in a newness of life which corresponds to the righteousness of God."[23]

Why do I talk about the repentance of Asian Americans? If one works with liberation from oppression as the ultimate goal of Asian Americans, oppressors would indeed be the sinners, and the oppressed would be more victims than sinners. But here I am working with the belief that there is an ultimate goal which includes but also transcends liberation. As mentioned earlier, the end for which God created the world and intelligent creatures is to repeat in time and space the internal communion of the trinitarian God. If one takes this larger framework for theological reflection, what is wrong with human beings is defined by a principle higher than the criterion of liberation and the oppressor–the oppressed dichotomy.

Sin or what is wrong with humanity, then, is defined in terms of whether or not human beings are in line with what God is doing in history. Sin in our context is the people's resistance to God's end in creation and failure to promote and participate in what God is doing here on earth. In this scheme, both the oppressors and the oppressed can be sinful to the extent they are alienated from God's own project in history.

The first sin we Asian Americans have to repent of is our attempt to avoid facing up to our liminal and marginalized predicament. It is disorienting and painful to face a situation of being "in-between" and of being marginalized. And it is almost human nature to try to run away from such a reality. Asian Americans' attempts to avoid their predicament take either the form of "nativism," in which we try to cling to our ethnic culture or enclave, or the form of "assimilationism," in which we try to think we are white. Nativism leads to self-ghettoization, which risks dangerous social and political isolation. Assimilationism can end up in severe disillusionment and despair. God calls us Asian Americans to be faithful to our Christian calling wherever we are actually located. If we avoid an honest awareness of where we are, we are avoiding our sacred calling.

We Asian Americans must also repent of our sin of self-hatred. The lowered self-image either about oneself or about one's ethnic group is, of course, the result of the internalization of the dominant group members' treatment of the members of one's ethnic group as inferior and deficient. When this happens to us Asian Americans, we are victims and not perpetrators. Nevertheless, to the extent that we Asian Americans let this prejudice become our own attitude and act out this self-hatred in relating to other Asian Americans, we are responsible for what we do. As Paul Tillich reminds us, sin is always tragic and also voluntary.[24] We are influenced by outside factors in our sins, but sins are also our own acts. We must repent of thinking that we as Asian Americans are somehow "less" than white people.

We Asian Americans also must repent of our own prejudices against African Americans and other minority groups. I can never forget witnessing an African American man being flatly refused service in a Korean restaurant. Some years ago, I entered a large Korean restaurant in a major U.S. city for a quick lunch. Almost as soon as I sat down at a table, a waitress came and took my order. Soon a well-dressed African American man came in and sat down at a table near me. I soon noticed that no one was coming to wait on him. This man waited over ten minutes and still no one came. Finally, he quietly got up and walked out. I still think I should have run after him and apologized to him for what had happened. I, of course, do not know how widespread such racist practices are in Korean American communities. I am not forgetting that many Korean and other Asian Americans, especially some churches, have made attempts to express a sense of solidarity with African American and other minority groups. Furthermore, I am aware of the highly complex nature of the relations between Asian Americans and other minority groups.[25] But still we Asian Americans must repent of any prejudice we may harbor toward persons of color.

In addition, we Asian Americans must confess our sin of worshiping idols and golden calves in this American wilderness. Asian Americans' lives are often driven by a materialistic version of the American Dream. Trying to send our children to Ivy League schools no matter what and other obsessions with worldly success are on the top of the list of golden calves we have been worshiping. Sending our children to good schools and achieving other forms of success are in themselves not wrong. But if we let these goals become obsessions, they overtake and control our lives.

Andrew Sung Park reminds us not to forget the sin of sexism in Korean American communities.[26] In spite of some gains in the status of women in Korea and other parts of the world, remnants of the age-old ideology of patriarchy and the consequent subordination and exploitation of women are still strongly present in Korea as well as in the Korean immigrant community. The situation is, of course, exacerbated by the frustration and anger Korean immigrants especially experienced in their early years in the United States due to their lack of cultural adaptation, the loss of the social status they had back home, and other difficulties.

Many Korean immigrants find it more convenient engaging in family-run small-business operations than looking for and maintaining jobs in American firms. Consequently, women become heavily engaged in their family stores and subject themselves to many hours of backbreaking labor. In addition, studies indicate, these women also do most of the housework with minimal assistance from their husbands.[27]

Another most shameful expression of patriarchal domination is spousal violence against women. A 1987 study of Korean immigrant women in Chicago showed shocking statistics. Of the 150 women who completed interviews, ninety (60 percent) reported being battered by their husbands. In terms of frequency, twenty-two (24 percent) of these battered women suffered from violence at least once a week, and thirty-four (37 percent) had been abused at least once a month. The women in this sample averaged thirty-six years of age and their average length of residence in the United States was five years. This study, therefore, does not indicate the degree of domestic violence among more settled Korean immigrants. But even by itself, this limited study is deeply disturbing.[28]

In churches also Asian American women face the barriers set up by patriarchy. They work in the kitchen and take care of many of the "small" chores while men hold the most powerful positions and make the official decisions. The most scandalous manifestation of sexism occurs at the time of the Lord's Supper. Usually, more than half of the congregation are women. Most of the time the ones who distribute the bread and wine are all men in white gloves. This happens in broad daylight and in the presence of many copies of the Bible which shout out the fact that it was usually women who served Jesus during his earthly ministry. Until the churches clean up their act, they can not say very much about the injustices in society.

Asian American churches must also repent of their failure to welcome and embrace persons of lower-income families and persons who are ostracized in their communities for some reason. Fumitaka Matsuoka remarks in his book *Out of Silence*: "Perhaps the severest critique we can direct upon Asian American churches is that to a certain extent they have co-opted into the very racist structure of society and thus have come to neglect the most alienated people in society, the poor and underclass, even among our own Asian Americans."[29]

Chapter 6
ASIAN AMERICAN IDENTITY AND THE CHRISTIAN FAITH

ASIAN AMERICAN IDENTITY IN A POSTMODERN AND POSTCOLONIAL CONTEXT

Postmodernism has stressed the thoroughly historical nature of human existence, and has made it impossible to think about human selves and their individual identities as things that are permanent and fixed. The identity or "who one is," therefore, is now spoken of as a dynamic reality that is constructed and reconstructed again and again. Stuart Hall points out that cultural identity is "a matter of 'becoming' as well as 'being.' . . . Cultural identities come from somewhere, and have histories. Like everything else which is historical, identities undergo constant transformation."[1]

While agreeing with the postmodernists in their rejection of the classical substance theory of the self and the modern foundationalist construal of self as transcendent mind, philosopher Paul Schrag believes that the jettisoning of the self understood in these senses does not entail the jettisoning of every sense of self. Schrag argues that in the aftermath of the postmodernist deconstruction of traditional metaphysics and epistemology, "a new self emerges, like the phoenix arising from its ashes—a praxis-oriented self," defined by the self's discourse, its actions, its being with others in the community. Schrag elaborates further on the unfixed character of identity by pointing out that one does not construct identity by patching together abstract ideas of cultural values. Identity, according to Schrag, is more like a "happening" that emerges as one speaks, makes decisions, carries out actions in relation to the others. Schrag explains, "it is only when one moves to the level of the discursive event, in which there is an effort to communicate something to someone, that the question 'Who is speaking?' takes on relevance and indeed becomes uncircumventable."[2]

So, the sense of identity emerges in and through actual discourse and action as the who of the discourse and the who of the action. What, then, constitutes the self's continuity and coherence? It is the narrative form, answers Schrag, that "comprises the continuing context, the expanding horizon of a retentional background and a protentional foreground, in which and against which our figures of discourse are called into being, play themselves out and conspire in the making of sense." What is true for human discourse applies also to human action. According to Schrag, "narrative is not simply the telling of a story by the who of discourse, providing a binding textuality of the past and future inscriptions; it is also the emplotment of a personal history through individual and institutional action."[3] Human actions are intelligible only when they are seen through the context of the narrative of a personal history. I will return below to the issue of narrative and identity.

While agreeing with postmodernism on the historical and thus continuously constructed nature of the identity of the human self, postcolonial studies have focused on the culturally hybrid identity of previously or presently colonized peoples. If one works with the assumption that there are "pure cultures," hybrid or racially mixed persons can be considered as strange and inferior to them. The concept of hybridity can, therefore, be used in a negative way.[4] But hybridity can also mean creativity and a new identity. Postcolonial writers, especially Homi Bhabha, have focused particularly on the hybrid identity and culture that emerge in the condition of being an immigrant, oppressed, or colonized minority. The culture of people in such conditions is "bafflingly both alike and different" from their parent or original culture. "It is something like 'culture's in-between,'" a culture's liminal and creative edge.[5] It is what Bhabha calls the "Third Space," as in the quotation below. In such situations, Bhabha argues, the colonized person's intentional construction of a hybrid identity and culture can be an activity of resistance to the dominant culture and also an act of forming a new identity and culture. This new identity and culture would be neither an accommodation to the dominant culture nor a culture inferior to it. In an oft-quoted passage, Bhabha writes:

> It is significant that the productive capacities of this Third Space have a colonial or postcolonial provenance. For a willingness to descend into that alien territory . . . may open the way to conceptualization of an international culture, based not on the exoticism of multiculturalism or the diversity of cultures, but on the inscription and articulation of culture's *hybridity*.[6]

In his 1966 essay entitled "Culture's In-Between," Bhabha explains further:

> In my own work I have developed the concept of hybridity to describe the construction of cultural authority within conditions of political antagonism or inequality. . . . Hybrid strategy . . . makes possible the emergence of an "interstitial" agency that refuses the binary representation of social antagonism. Hybrid agencies find their voice in a dialectic that does not seek cultural supremacy or sovereignty. They deploy the partial culture from which they emerge to construct visions of community, and versions of historic memory, that give narrative form to the minority positions they occupy; the outside of the inside: the part in the whole.[7]

What Bhabha calls "the partial culture" in the above quotation is the culture of a marginalized ethnic minority that is "bafflingly alike and different" from either the dominant culture of the society where they presently live or the culture of their ethnic or ancestral origin.[8] Such a minority culture is a "partial culture" in comparison to the cultures that have been around for a long time and that are the "total culture" of a people or a society. Bhabha also calls the "partial culture" of a minority group "culture's in-between," culture's creative opening for change.

Bhabha believes that, in a colonized or oppressed condition, the oppressed group can embrace the creative space of their in-betweenness, and that in that "Third Space" they can work with their "partial" or mixed culture to construct a hybrid culture and identity that have an integrity of their own and are distinguishable from either the oppressor's culture or the culture of their origin. What emerges from the "Third Space" is a new identity.[9] In other words, the newly constructed hybrid identity has an integrity of its own, and resists the hegemony of either side of the binary of white American vs. nonwhite Asian. "Asian American" is different from white American and from Asian, but is not for that reason deficient or inferior. So Bhabha's "interstitial agency," noted above, is an agency of resistance. The liminal space in which hybrid identity is constructed is a site of resistance to hegemony of any one of the diverse elements out of which Asian American identity is constructed.

WORKING ON ASIAN AMERICAN IDENTITY

What does it mean for Asian Americans to construct a hybrid "Asian American" identity in the liminal space of in-betweenness in which we live? Bhabha's idea of hybridization in the "Third Space" of in-betweenness is a general concept that can be utilized appropriately only if we keep in mind the particular nature of our liminal situation in the United States.

To construct a hybrid Asian American identity in American society is, first of all, to resist the essentialized idea either of America or Asia. The Eurocentric idea of America has been essentialized—that is, made into a permanent truth. Even if Asian Americans have names like Peter and David, or Mary and Sarah, and speak an impeccable English, they are still asked, "Where are you from?" If one is not a white person, he or she is simply not considered as a "real American" in this country.

To affirm that Asian Americans are Americans is an act of rejecting and resisting the dominant group's notion that only European Americans are "real Americans." The term *American* includes Native Americans, African Americans, Hispanic Americans, English Americans, Italian Americans, and many others. To construct an Asian American identity is to embrace all these different kinds of Americans in our own conception of ourselves. The cultures and histories of the peoples of all the different ancestral backgrounds cannot be, in a mechanical way, the material content of what constitutes the Asian American identity. But none of those peoples can be excluded from the meaning of an Asian American identity. What this means is that Asian American identity could appropriate as our own some aspect of the cultures of all the peoples who belong to America, and that Asian American identity must be permanently open.

A couple of decades ago I was teaching a course on the theologies of marginalized peoples. One day in class, an African American student raised his hand and asked, "Dr. Lee, what do you mean by the term *American* whenever you use the term *Asian American*? Are you sure you don't mean 'white American' by the word *American*?" I just about jumped out of my chair. It did not take me long to realize for the first time that I always had in mind "Asian- white American" whenever I used the term *Asian American*. I had been excluding that African American student from the meaning of the term *American*. I had been excluding the long history of African Americans' suffering and their struggles for freedom and human dignity from what constitutes American history. I confessed to the student and the class that I had been living with the idea of white Americans as the "real Americans," and that I would never do it again.

Some Asian Americans may internalize the idea of European Americans as "real Americans." When this happens, Asian Americans will try to "out-white" the whites. But this strategy is bound to fail because, as noted in chapter 1, the whites will not accept nonwhite persons as one of them. For nonwhite people, social or structural assimilation does not follow cultural assimilation. To construct an Asian American identity, then, is to resist the idea of European Americans as "real Americans," both as an idea prevalent in American society and also as an internalized idea in the minds of Asian Americans themselves.

To construct Asian American identity, therefore, is a work of reconstructing or of restoring the meaning of America itself. In fact, Asian Americans who struggled for justice and human rights in the past did so by appealing to the fundamental principles upon which this nation itself was founded. By doing so, Asian Americans endeavored to restore or reconstruct the meaning of America. Japanese Americans' struggle against the injustice of their internment during World War II was based upon the principles of the U.S. Constitution. The Fair Play Committee at Heart Mountain concentration camp argued that "drafting Nisei from these concentration camps, without restoration of their civil rights and rectification of the tremendous economic losses suffered by them, was not only morally wrong, but legally questionable." Gary Y. Okihiro points out further that "the Asian American struggle for inclusion within the American community, as migrants and citizens, was principally based upon the guarantee of equal protection under the Fourteenth Amendment."[10] Okihiro observes in his book *Margins and Mainstreams: Asians in American History and Culture,*

> And despite its authorship of the central tenets of democracy, the mainstream has been silent on the publication of its creed. In fact, the margin has held the nation together with its expansive reach; the margin has tested and ensured the guarantees of citizenship; and the margin has been the true defender of American democracy, equality, liberty. From that vantage, we can see the margin as mainstream.[11]

In telling the story of how Asian Americans and other minorities have contributed to the work of calling to America's attention its true ideals and goals, Okihiro is constructing a history of Asian Americans. What is usually presented as "American history" does not contain the full history of Asian Americans. Asian Americans are invisible in the history of the country in which they have lived and labored. One telling example is the official photograph of the people gathered to celebrate the completion of the first Transcontinental Railroad across America. Although thousands of Chinese workers were the people who built that railroad, not a single Chinese person can be found in that photograph.[12]

To construct one's identity is to make a connection between one's past, present, and future. Without a past, one cannot understand one's present and cannot move ahead into the future. Asian Americans' construction of their identity, therefore, includes the work of excavating out of America's past the history of Asian Americans. I shall return to the role of the past in the construction of Asian American identity when I discuss the narrative character of identity.

Together with America, Asia is the other primary factor in Asian Americans' construction of their identity. For first-generation Asian immigrants, Asia, or more specifically their home country, is vividly a part of them. But even for Asian Americans of the younger generations, even if they have never visited their ancestral home country, Asia is still a part of them in small and yet real ways: in their diet, in their physical appearance, in the stories their parents or grandparents tell them or in yet other ways.

In appropriating Asia, just as in the case of America, Asian Americans have to resist the essentialized idea of the "real Asian." Asia does not stand still but constantly changes. Some culturally conservative first-generation Korean men's insistence that patriarchy is an element of "real Asianness" must be resisted. The top-down style of parental authority as true Asianness also must be resisted. There is no eternally fixed idea of what it means to be Asian.

Just as the idea of an essentialized Asia must be resisted, it must also be acknowledged that there is never an uninterpreted Asia. In constructing Asian American identity, Asian Americans must resist any interpretations of Asia that are unjust. What I have in mind is the historical fact that Western Christian missionaries brought to various parts of Asia not only the Christian gospel and modernization but also a negative perspective on Asian cultural and religious traditions. In many cases, Asians who embraced the Christian gospel also bought the Western prejudice that some aspects of Asian culture and religions are all pagan and idolatrous practices to be rejected by Christian converts.

In Korea, for example, Christians have done away with the annual family rituals in which the deceased members are remembered and prayers are offered to ancestors requesting their blessing. The rituals certainly contain some elements that involve religious reverence of the ancestors. Therefore, Korean Christian churches certainly may find those religious aspects objectionable. But the entire ceremony did not have to be pronounced idolatrous and banned for church members. Christian churches could have modified the traditional ritual in such a way that those parts which give the appearance of a "worship" of ancestors could be taken out. Then they could have reinterpreted the ritual as a time of remembering and celebrating the family's continuing spiritual unity and communion with the deceased. Such a reinterpreted ancestor ritual could be grounded on the Christian belief in the communion of saints, saints here on earth and in heaven.

The ancestor ritual involves bowing in front of the photos or names of the deceased. This practice has been condemned as idolatrous, but it does not have to be seen in such a way. Bowing to other persons in Korean, as in many other Asian countries, is a ubiquitous gesture of respect and affection for the other person. And Koreans bow to other persons in all kinds of circumstances and at all kinds of places. Some years ago, when I was visiting Korea, I met a Korean Presbyterian elder of around seventy years of age. He told me that he had many brothers and sisters, but he was the only Christian in his family. And at the ancestor ritual time for his family, everyone would bow in front of the pictures of the deceased parents and grandparents. Everyone, that is, except him, a Presbyterian elder. He alone remained standing. And with a deep sadness, and tears welling in his aging eyes, he told me that at times like that, he would feel that every cell in his body was saying, "Bow, Bow, Bow!" I took his hands in mine, and repeated to him softly but firmly, "Next time, be sure to bow, not to worship, but out of respect, bow. You have bowed a million times to all kinds of persons. What could possibly be wrong if you bowed to your deceased parents and grandparents out of respect and affection?" What, indeed, could be wrong with honoring one's ancestors? So Asian Americans reinterpret Asia as we think of Asia in constructing and reconstructing our hybrid identity in the liminal space between Asia and America.

FAITH AND IDENTITY

How is Christian faith related to Asian Americans' identity construction? What difference does Asian American Christians' faith make in the construction of their identity?

The most fundamental way faith is related to identity construction for Asian Americans is that it provides the courage to face the bewildering space of liminality and to do the work of constructing a hybrid identity without relying upon the false security of an essentialized finite principle. Faith is the act of trusting and embracing God's unconditional acceptance of us as God's children. Faith, therefore, is the unshakable foundation of one's sense of dignity and self-esteem. In faith, one affirms the meaningfulness and moral worth of oneself and one's existence. In and through faith, one stands firm even if the world considers her or him as one without value and worth.

Faith, therefore, is the source of the courage not to be shaken by the uncertain and bewildering space of liminality. Faith is the courage to refuse the temptation to absolutize any one of the finite factors in identity construction and thereby to set up a false source of security.

Fumitaka Matsuoka calls Asian Americans' experience of liminality an experience of "holy insecurity." "To embrace the 'holy insecurity' of a life, or being *jook sing* [the Cantonese word for a piece of empty bamboo with no roots at either end], that defies any conventional definition," writes Matsuoka, "means to receive the gift of courage to live in the midst of an unresolved and often ambiguous state of life."[13] So faith is the courage to be liminal, to be in the state of "holy insecurity" of in-betweenness and to do the work of identity construction in that liminal space.

"Interstitial integrity" is what Rita Nakashima Brock calls the ability to construct one's hybrid identity in a liminal space in which the dominance of any of the factors is not tolerated. Interstitial integrity, therefore, forges an identity without abolishing the ambiguity and openness of the liminal situation of a hybrid identity. In this way, Brock explains, interstitial integrity "allows space for the multiple social locations of identity in a multicultural context."[14]

According to Brock, interstitial integrity is a creative energy that insists on "holding the many in one." In a 2007 essay, entitled "Cooking without Recipes," Brock writes:

> Interstitial integrity is our ability to lie down, spread-eagled, reaching to all the many worlds we have known, all the memories we have been given, tempered in the cauldrons of history and geography in our one body. We find our value in taking our small place in long legacies of incarnating spirit in bodies. Through such legacies, we participate in shaping our many worlds, and we grow in wisdom and beauty and live in the traces we leave in others, so they, too, might cook without recipes.[15]

Interstitial integrity is also integration, Brock says, in that it has its own "moments of entireness," and such a moment of entireness is accompanied by the conviction that such an integration, though hybrid in nature, is not "a state of being impaired or lesser than one whose identity is monocultural."[16]

Another important point that Brock makes is that interstitial integrity is not simply the ability to cope with the experience of being liminal and peripheral. Interstitial integrity is more. It is the work of "making meaning out of multiple worlds by refusing to disconnect from any one of them, while not pledging alliance to a singular one."[17]

"Interstitial integrity" is the courage to refuse to consider any one "moment of entireness" or integration of various parts of oneself as one's final identity. Brock explains: "this refusal to rest in one place, to reject a narrowing of who we are by either/or decisions, or to be placed always on the periphery, is interstitial integrity."[18]

If faith is the source of the moral strength to face the liminal space and to do the work of identity construction in that space, or the ability to maintain an "interstitial integrity," does faith also make any material difference to the content of the hybrid Asian American identity itself? From where or what does identity construction attain a direction, intentionality, and meaningfulness? The answer, I believe, is that a connection between identity construction and the Christian faith is possible because of the inherently narrative character of both. It is in the form of a narrative that self or identity is given continuity, direction, and purposefulness.

IDENTITY AND NARRATIVE

I earlier briefly mentioned Paul Schrag's argument that narrative gives human discourse and action a unity. It is Stephen Crites, however, in his seminal 1971 essay "The Narrative Quality of Experience," who pointed out that the very nature of human experience in time is inherently narrative in form. The present moment contains the modality of the past which is determinate and the modality of the future which is indeterminate. How can there be, then, a unity of experi-

ence that embraces both the determinateness of the past and the inde-
terminateness of the future?

Crites's thesis is that "the tensed unity of these modalities requires
narrative form both for its expression . . . and for its own sense of the
meaning of its internal coherence." Expanding further on this point,
Crites says, "But this incipient story, implicit in the very possibility of
experience, must be such that it can absorb both the chronicle of memory and the scenario of anticipation, absorb them within a richer narrative form without effacing the difference between the determinacy of
the one and the indeterminacy of the other."[19] So "narrative alone can
contain the full temporality of experience in a unity of form" and do so
without abolishing the distinctiveness of the past and the future. Narrative alone can give time a unity and meaning both in human experience as such and also in personal identity.

A human self is ineluctably in history, with past, present, and
future. The sense of who one is or a person's identity, then, has to make
sense out of one's personal history as a whole. Since history is narrative
in form, a person's sense of himself or herself as a whole has to take a
narrative form that can hold the three tenses together. As what constitutes the unity of one's sense of who one is, narrative gives his or her
self coherence and a sense of direction. It is then at this basic level of
the self that the Christian faith in narrative form can have its impact
and influence. It is as a narrative that the Christian faith has a material
influence in and upon human selves.

The Christian tradition is largely in the narrative form. The Story
of God, or what Crites calls "the Story within the story," is that the
triune God, whose essence is the eternal disposition to repeat loving community and beauty, creates the world to repeat in time God's
internal communion and beauty and creates human beings to participate in this project of God. The stories of Israel, and the story of the
incarnate Son of God Jesus Christ, are the central biblical stories that
tell of God's actions in and through the people of Israel and his incarnate Son.

Many Asian Americans live with the materialistic American Dream story as the narrative that gives their identity a unity and a direction. If an Asian American or an Asian immigrant fails to achieve the American Dream as he or she understands it, and if he or she begins to doubt whether that story is what should govern their lives, they then face a crisis. Such a crisis as this could also be brought about by hearing other stories, such as the Christian stories, which govern some other people's lives in the United States. This crisis has to do with the unity of the person as a self and the direction of his or her life itself. The old American Dream story may not work anymore, and there is no other story ready at hand to replace it. What is needed is a new story that he or she can appropriate as his or her own. The new story will have to be able to bind together the past, present, and future into a whole and some pattern that is meaningful to him or her. Until a new story takes over as the unifying principle of his or her identity, she or he is in a liminal situation. The liminality of this crisis enables a person to be more open to what is new than he or she might usually be.

If the person, spoken of above, encounters the Christian story (the story of God, the story of Jesus, and the stories of believers) and appropriates it as his or her own, a conversion takes place. For the Christian story to be truly appropriated, the person must know intellectually the Christian narratives but must live out the Christian story in his or her personal and social existence.

An Asian American Christian who is still pursuing the materialistic American Dream, for instance, could be challenged by the narrative of Abraham. In Hebrews 11, we read the following narrative:

> By faith Abraham obeyed when he was called to set out for a place that he was to receive as an inheritance; and he set out, not knowing where he was going. . . . For he looked to the city that has foundations, whose architect and builder is God. . . . They confessed that they were strangers and foreigners on the earth, for people who speak in this way make it clear that they are seeking a homeland. If they had been

thinking of the land that they had left behind, they would have had opportunity to return. But as it is, they desire a better country, that is, a heavenly one. Therefore God is not ashamed to be called their God; indeed, he has prepared a city for them. (Heb. 11:8, 10, 13-16)

First of all, the term *heavenly* does not need to be taken as referring to an other-worldly place. Abraham and his descendants were in fact strangers and foreigners in the land of Canaan (Gen. 23:4; Ps. 39:12) and so understood themselves as such. The "better country" Abraham was in search of is not some place beyond history but an actual historical reality that he and his descendants can work for as a concrete historical reality.[20]

Abraham's story is particularly pertinent to Asian immigrants who may be wondering what the meaning of their existence in this country is. Abraham's story can be interpreted as saying that now that the Asian immigrants have left home and are here in America, it is an opportunity to take up the pilgrimage toward "a better country" and work to make America a country that is more according to God's will. Their situation can be seen as a calling to live as the creative minority in America. Moreover, if Asian American Christians appropriate Abraham's story as their own, they might see their life's goal as being to continue to live here "as strangers and foreigners" and work to build a "better America," "whose architect and builder is God." In this way, their Christian faith would have something to do with their identity and their life as marginalized and liminal people in America.

Chapter 7

ASIAN AMERICAN CHURCH

Asian American church as a Christian church is the community of liminal and marginalized Asian Americans who have experienced the God of unconditional acceptance and love through the transforming experience of *communitas* with Jesus Christ in the power of the Holy Spirit. By that experience they have been empowered to live in their liminality and to exercise their liminal creativity in pursuit of the realization of the reign of God here on earth. The Asian American church has its roots in the liminal and marginalized people whom the God of Abraham, Isaac, and Jacob called into being as God's "servant people." The Asian American church as a Christian church has its roots also in the new "family of God" into which Jesus Christ in his earthly ministry gathered those liminal and marginalized Galileans and others who experienced *communitas* with him. The Asian American church as a Christian church is also connected with the everlasting city in which God's people will be gathered "before the throne and before the Lamb" "from every nation, from all tribes and peoples and languages" (Rev. 7:9). It should be pointed out that making these assertions is deeply humbling in light of the serious imperfections of the Christian church as a whole and of the Asian American church in particular. It is the mystery of the church, however, that, in spite of its failings and weaknesses, the risen and exalted Christ is its head and is working in and through it to promote God's own project of repeating God's love and beauty in time and space.

CHURCH AS *COMMUNITAS* AND STRUCTURE

Victor Turner makes a distinction between "spontaneous or existential *communitas*" and "normative *communitas*." The immediate experience of *communitas* is the "spontaneous or existential *communitas*." *Communitas*, however, is transient and has to give way to structure. "Communitas itself soon develops a structure," Turner writes, "in which free relationships between individuals become converted into norm-governed relationships between social personae." The "normative communitas," Turner explains further, "is where, under the influence of time, the need to mobilize and organize resources, and the necessity of social control among members in pursuance of these goals, the existential communitas is organized into a perduring social system." Another term Turner introduces is "ideological *communitas*," by which he means "the formulation of remembered attributes of the communitas experience in the form of a utopian blueprint for the form of society."[1]

In light of ideological *communitas*, normative *communitas* is always inadequate. When spontaneous *communitas* evolves into a structure, those originally involved in the spontaneous *communitas* would attempt to have the features of spontaneous *communitas* be reflected in the structure. But as Turner points out, "spontaneous communitas can never be adequately expressed in a structural form."[2] From our theological perspective, however, we would not wish to say that spontaneous *communitas* is "never" adequately expressed in a structural form. Asian American theology must speak eschatologically about the day when God the Father, God the Son, and God the Holy Spirit will bring about "a new heaven and a new earth" in which there will be no gap between *communitas* and structure. But on this side of the eschaton, the church as an institution can never completely reflect and express spontaneous *communitas*. Turner states further: "Structural action swiftly becomes arid and mechanical if those involved in it are not periodically immersed in the regenerative abyss of communitas."[3] In other words, for normative *communitas* to express the features of *communitas* (e.g., egalitarian relations between persons), the persons in a structure must from time to time be immersed in the experience of spontaneous *communitas*.

To use Turner's terminology, then, the church is both *communitas* and structure, or a dialectic between structure and *communitas*. Turner defines structure as "the patterned arrangements of role sets, status sets, and status sequences consciously recognized and regularly operative in a given society and closely bound up with legal and practical norms and sanctions."[4] Structures are not imposed upon *communitas*; rather, *communitas* inevitably develops a structure, because "communitas cannot stand alone if the material and organizational needs of human beings are to be adequately met."[5] *Communitas* and structure, according to Turner, must maintain "the appropriate relationship" between them "under the given circumstances of time and place, to accept each modality when it is paramount without rejecting the other, and not to cling to one when its present impetus is spent."[6] As pointed out above, structure, according to Turner, becomes mechanical if the spirit of *communitas* is not periodically instilled into it. On the other hand, the almost "magical" power of *communitas* alone without "lucid thought and sustained will" cannot be "readily applied to the organizational details of social existence."[7]

So human society is both *communitas* and structure. I borrow Turner's concepts to think of Asian American church as both *communitas* and structure. In regard to an understanding of the church as *communitas* and structure, three observations need to be made.

1. The Asian American church conceived of as *communitas* and also structure can avoid the pitfalls of overemphasizing one at the expense of the other. Avery Dulles, in his book, *Models of*

the Church, discusses as the first two of the five models "Church as Institution" and "Church as Mystical Communion." Dulles points out that, on the one hand, an exclusive emphasis upon structure leads to institutionalism in which church as an institution exists for its own sake, and to clericalism in which the laity is left behind in passivity. If communion among church members is overemphasized, on the other hand, the church may become self-contained and distant from the larger world. According to Turner, "communitas *itself* soon develops a structure."[8] *Communitas* and structure go together.

2. Church is both *communitas* and structure, but *communitas* is primary. Turner wrote: "It [*communitas*] is the *fons et origo* of all structures and at the same time their critique."[9] For the Asian American church, too, *communitas* is the origin of its structure. As Avery Dulles points out, however, the church as community is more than a community of human believers. The church has a vertical dimension as well—namely, the believers' communion with the incarnate Son of God, Jesus Christ.[10] Historically speaking, the church is to be traced back to the small group of Galilean followers of Jesus. At the same time, the community of Jesus and his followers originates from and repeats in time and space the eternal communion in the internal life of the triune God.

The communal nature of the church is particularly important in the Asian American context because of the social isolation Asian Americans experience in American society at large. But the importance of the church as a community for Asian American Christians is all the more reason for not letting the church become a cozy social gathering that is detached from the rest of the world. An overemphasis upon church as community at the expense of structure can also lead to procedural and organizational chaos or crisis.

3. An appropriate emphasis upon church as structure implies the church's responsibility to be concerned about society at large. According to Turner, *communitas* inevitably gives way to structure. Without structure and procedures, *communitas* cannot meet the human needs for organization. Now it would appear to be true that the structure which *communitas* acquires cannot but be connected to and be within the larger framework of the structure of the society as a whole in which the church's structure is located. The church as structure is connected to the city's water system and other infrastructure of the society. The church depends upon the police and fire departments. The members of the church individually participate in the election of the leaders of the society. The church as an institution, therefore, is ineluctably connected with the larger world. The church and the society it is in, then, will inevitably influence each other. The church must decide if it is going to let itself totally be influenced by the society or if it is going to challenge the society at times in terms of its own values as a community of Jesus Christ. I will return to this point below.

ASIAN AMERICAN CHURCH AS REFUGE AND LIMINAL SPACE

For the liminal and marginalized Asian Americans, the Asian American church serves as refuge where they find comfort, encouragement, and aid. The service that Asian immigrant churches have rendered to newly arrived Asian immigrants has been indispensable for their sheer survival during the first several months in their newly adopted country.[11] The Asian American church is also a place of aid and comfort for those who have been here for many years. Throughout the week, they endure the cold stares, subtle and not-so-subtle put-downs, and other indignities. They come to Asian American churches on Sundays, and they find themselves fitting in. The fact that no one asks, "Where are you from?," is a great relief. It is as if every cell in the body relaxes and is pleased simply to be at a place where everyone else is like oneself.

So the Asian American church as a refuge is a place of healing. And no one can deny that such a restorative effect which the Asian American church has on its members is an important function of the church. But the Asian American church's refuge function is a good thing only to a certain point. If refuge becomes a place of escape, church as refuge functions as something that is detrimental to the church's being church. Seeking comfort in church as a refuge sometimes is an expression of some Asian immigrants' reluctance to face up to the challenges of their new environment by clinging to the ways of their home country. They insist on singing the songs, praying the prayers, and preaching the sermons they used to sing, pray, and preach in their home country. They resist any changes with the remark, "That's not the way we used to do it back home." Such an escapist nationalism is tragicomic because Asian immigrants' homelands in Asia do not stand still but change everyday.

An Asian American church which is willing to face the challenges that its members face in America needs to see itself as a space of liminality and not only as a refuge. For one thing, the members of Asian American churches live in a *de facto* liminal situation in the United States. And if the church is going to minister to them, it must itself be a liminal place. The other reason why the church must be a space of liminality has to with the very nature of Asian American church's being a church. From Asian American theology's perspective, the church's very own being originated in a liminal space—in the redeeming experience of *communitas* with God in Jesus in the infinite liminal space of his cross. And it is the church's fundamental task to remember and reenact the life-changing experience of the original *communitas* experience in the liminal space of the cross.

The weekly Sunday worship in an Asian American church can be an experience of liminality and *communitas*. The participants in worship are at least relatively freed from their social roles and social status and their place in the social hierarchy. The sermons, hymns, and prayers

could also be designed to evoke in the participants a sense of their liminality. Moreover, the members' sense of being liminal in American life
could be brought out to a more explicit consciousness and reinforce
the sense of liminal space in worship. In daily life, Asian Americans'
de facto liminality usually remains dormant under their consciousness
and they are not personally aware of it as their existential issue. The
worship time in the church, where they enjoy group approval, can
provide Asian Americans a reasonably "safe place," or what Robert L.
Moore called "containment," in which they can allow themselves to be
explicitly aware of the liminal and marginalized existence they lead in
American society.[12] In this way, the liminality Asian Americans experiences in their churches is directly related with the most basic existential
issue they must face in their lives in America. The direct connection
between Asian Americans' liminality in society and their liminality in
church would mean that what happens in the church can have a great
impact on the way Asian Americans conduct their daily lives.

Timothy L. Carson has pointed out that worship, if it is not suf-
ficiently freed from hierarchy and status, degenerates into a mere
ceremony that reinforces the existing social and cultural structure.[13]
Some worship services, especially those in which church officers are
ordained and installed, display so much hierarchy in the church and
the society that they cannot be called the kind of ritual that changes
lives. Life-changing worship as a ritual has to be genuinely liminal.
Those ceremonies of ordination and installation need to be seriously
rethought and should be carried out differently.

The sacrament of the Lord's Supper is a time in the life of the
church when liminality and the reenactment of transforming *communitas* with God's love in Jesus can be most powerfully experienced.
Everyone comes to the Lord's table with the knowledge that they are
all equal in being sinners in need of forgiveness and healing before
God. Certainly, at the time of the Lord's Supper, all participants must
leave behind them, at least temporarily, their social roles and social
status.

In the Korean American churches with which I am most familiar, however, the Lord's Supper is often a time when the intrachurch dynamics and social status and hierarchy are most visibly displayed. Only the male elders and the minister in black suits and white gloves handle the white linen and the shiny plates and the sacramental elements, the bread and wine. The deacons and other church members sit in their pews waiting for the elders to bring bread and wine to them. In circumstances such as this, the church members are more likely to be thinking about the church hierarchy rather than the meaning of the sacrament. To be elected an elder, for many Korean American church men, is the highest status they can achieve in the Korean American community. "Will I ever be elected an elder and be able to serve communion in the church?," these men are likely to be thinking. There are certainly more egalitarian ways of conducting the Lord's Supper, and many churches are practicing such an approach so that status and roles are made less visible and the chances for liminal time and *communitas* become greater. Unless some steps are taken to make the Lord's Supper freer from hierarchy and status, it is in danger of turning into mere ceremonies that reinforce the existing church's and society's structures.

More than a couple of decades ago, I attended the annual meeting of the National Presbyterian Council, the national gathering of all Korean American churches belonging to the Presbyterian Church (USA). More than five hundred Korean American clergy and lay leaders were at this great meeting. First on the program was the opening worship service with the Lord's Supper. I was coming down the long escalator to go to the auditorium where worship was to be held. I noticed many circles of Korean American clergypersons in the hallway excitedly greeting each other and enjoying being together. There was also a lone, tall, white gentleman, whom I recognized as a very prominent denominational leader, whom I will call Dr. S. He was wandering slowly around those Korean American clergy circles, but no one paid him any attention. Even if anyone recognized him, the pastors did not seem to be ready to open up their circles and welcome him. He just walked around the hallway waiting for the people to start going into the auditorium for the opening worship.

I was sitting in the front part of the large group in the auditorium, and at one point got up to look back. I noticed Dr. S. sitting all by himself smack in the middle of five-hundred-plus Korean American clergy. He must have felt that for the time being he had left the structure, hierarchy, and certainly his social status in the denomination and American society. But then the Korean American ministers who surrounded him were also strangers and aliens in their newly adopted country, not fully belonging either to their homeland in Asia or to their new adopted country, America.

The leaders of the worship and those conducting the Lord's Supper also did not exhibit much hierarchy. They all seemed as though they were local pastors in our host city. This gathering clearly was a liminal space, an in-between place, where people had left their ecclesial and social structure at least for a while. Those who served the communion also helped foster an egalitarian atmosphere.

After the service, I went to my room upstairs and later came down again to see some people. As I was coming down the same long escalator, I noticed again circles of Korean American pastors, this time talking to each other even more excitedly and jovially than they did before the service. But I did not see Dr. S. wandering around the hallway. He was in one of the Korean American pastoral circles, talking with them excitedly and waving his long arms. *Communitas* had occurred.

Commenting on the essential marks of the church, John Calvin wrote: "Wherever we see the Word of God purely preached and heard, and the sacraments administered according to Christ's institution, there, it is not to be doubted, a church of God exists."[14] Preaching of the word and administration of the sacraments are essential to the being of the church in Asian American theology, too. I would have to add, however, that in a church, preaching, administering the sacraments, and all other things need to be done in such a way that they bring the congregation into the infinite space of liminality and the redeeming experience of *communitas* with God in Jesus Christ.

THE PROPHETIC MINISTRY OF ASIAN AMERICAN CHURCHES

Why Do Many Asian American Churches Shy Away from Their Prophetic Role?

To be located socially in the in-between space of liminality between two or more worlds is also to be located at the edge or periphery of both of those worlds. And to be located at a peripheral space is conducive to a prophetic critique of, and resistance to, the dominant center. The Asian American church, located socially and culturally at the periphery of American society, has as one of its central callings the prophetic critique of, and resistance to, the racist culture and practices of the dominant group in America.

But why is it that most Asian American churches—with quite a few exceptions, I am sure—are reluctant to be involved in the issues emerging from the world at large? One reason is the still-persisting influence of St. Augustine's *City of God* in which the city of God and the city of man [*sic*] are sharply distinguished. The church has to do with the spiritual realm of God and not with the mundane matters of human society. The "things of Caesar" and the "things of God" are not to be mixed. The traditional association of religion with the Platonic conception of soul as not only distinguishable but also separable from body has only deepened the dichotomy between the transcendent and the this-worldly realms.

The second reason for the church-world dichotomy is the interpretation of the Bible as teaching passivity in regard to worldly matters. One is reminded of Jesus' statements such as: "Do not resist an evildoer. But if any one strikes you on the right cheek, turn the other also" (Matt. 5:39); "Give to the emperor the things that are the emperor's, and to God the things that are God's" (Mark 12:17). A careful exegesis of these statements will show that Jesus was not recommending a passive attitude to an evil that is done to a person.[15] But Jesus' statements have been taken simplistically for so long as meaning a passive attitude to all political matters.

The third reason for many Asian American churches' apolitical stance has to do with the individualistic conception of faith that many of their ministers and members have. The emphasis is on the "personal relationship with God." There is absolutely nothing wrong with this emphasis. The problem is that often such a relationship is taken as not including many other kinds of relationships—for example, relationship with one's neighbors, relationship with God's creation, and so forth. What matters is that one "accepts Jesus Christ as one's personal Savior and Lord," and then one stops right at that point. Practicing what one believes, taking care of the world that God created through Christ, showing one's concern about all other persons who are also the brothers and sisters of Jesus Christ—these and other important matters are not stressed. Everything seems to stop with the act of accepting Christ. That is indeed the central and indispensable act of a Christian, but that act contains or implies so many other actions.

There is still another reason why most members of Asian American churches are reluctant to see their churches get involved with political issues. Sociological studies have shown that one of the several reasons why many Korean immigrants choose to attend church is because being associated with churches is considered as "being American." So belonging to a church is related to the immigrants' desire to be "accepted" by the American public and to belong to "mainstream America." Persons who are anxious to be regarded as "good Americans" are not going to be willing to express any criticism of American society. These persons and their churches would naturally tend to be apolitical.

In chapter 4, I discussed how Jesus spoke vigorously against the political and the religious authorities that were exploiting the village peasants. Jesus' attitude toward political engagement was not one of passivity but, rather, a nonviolent resistance against all forms of injustice and oppression.[16]

A hopeful development in recent years is that some evangelical younger-generation Asian American church leaders are calling for the church's paying greater attention to justice issues. Theologian Peter Cha, for example, writes about how his reflections on the 1992 Los Angeles uprising, when many Korean American businesses were targeted by African American rioters, have made him keenly aware of the matter of justice facing the church. Speaking specifically of the Korean American church's work of reconciliation with African American brothers and sisters, Cha writes: "It was becoming clearer that this ministry of reconciliation required the church's commitment to the Biblical understanding of social justice, that calls God's people to identify with the poor and the marginalized and to seek justice on their behalf."[17]

Equally noteworthy is Asian American pastor David Gibbons's pilgrimage of discovering the central place of justice in the gospel of Jesus Christ. Gibbons is the founding pastor of the evangelical and multiethnic Asian American church New Song Community Church, in Irvine, California. Under his leadership, New Song has launched large-scale ministries of social justice and racial reconciliation.

In search of an understanding of the place of justice issues in the church, Gibbons turned first to the Bible itself. Gibbons confesses, "I knew the call for justice was in the Bible, but didn't know that it was this clear." He told his congregation: "I feel that this [social justice] is at the very heart of God, and if we don't do this, then we are not embracing the whole gospel." Gibbons comments further: "I think the church received the call to social justice well because it has a high view of Scripture. . . . I don't think any one can argue against it from a biblical perspective; it's just too clear."[18] It is a good thing that both Cha and Gibbons discovered the centrality of God's call for justice in the Bible. Most Asian American Christians have a high view of the Bible, so perhaps the call for justice will make just as strong an impression on them as it did on Cha and Gibbons.

The church, of course, should not engage in such partisan politics as endorsing specific candidates. For one thing, the democratic process of competition among candidates should be respected by the churches. Further, the members of a congregation may have different views, and their differences of opinion should be respected. Theologically speaking, the church should not influence the public on how to vote when the church itself has no way of attaining a complete certainty as to the qualities of individual candidates.

Prophetic Ministry to the World from the Periphery

Jesus spoke prophetically against the oppressive and exploitative practices of the Roman Empire and the Jerusalem Temple. Jesus' prophetic position was at the periphery or, in Richard Rohr's phrase, "the edge of the inside." The church is ineluctably inside the world. Whether the church is in or outside the world is not an appropriate question. The church should be both inside and at the edge of the world. The Asian American church's social location is *de facto* the edge or periphery of the world.

In relating to the world from the periphery of the inside of the world, there are several advantages:[19]

1. Since the church at the periphery is not tied to the ideas of the dominant or mainline group, it can suggest to the dominant group ideas and possibilities that the dominant group cannot come up with on its own. If the idea suggested by the church is critical or subversive of the dominant group, the church may indeed be criticized in return or even be oppressed or persecuted. The church must always be willing to take such risks.

2. If the church is willing to stay independent from the prevailing values and imperatives of the dominant group, the church can avoid a situation when it will have to act against its own principles in order to go along with the prevailing values of the dominant group. The church can hold its own system of values

if it maintains a certain distance from the mainline groups of
society and remain at the periphery.

3. If the church is at the periphery and not at the center of the
dominant group, then it does not end up having to carry out the
agenda of the society's dominant group. The internal pressures
of the dominant group would be hard to resist for a church that
is part of it, and the church would completely forfeit its real
mission. In order to preserve the integrity of the church's true
mission, the church has to be located at the periphery of the
society though not out of it. If the church were totally out of
society (not in the world), it would become irrelevant to society
and the world.

4. If the dominant group oppresses or attacks the church, the
church at the periphery would have the possibility of not react-
ing in "an eye for an eye, a tooth for a tooth" principle of fight-
ing evil with evil, and thereby becoming just the same as the
enemy. The church and its members at the periphery will be
able to keep their own perspective on things and resist evil in
a way that does not perpetuate evil. By being on the periphery, a church and its individual members have the ability and
freedom to respond to evil on terms other than those that the
aggressor defines. By operating from the periphery, the church
can resist evil without becoming like the oppressor and without
selling out its own system of values and perspective on life.

5. The church's peripheral location enables it to establish a solidarity with those who are marginalized. The ministry with
and for the poor, the sick, and the oppressed is a particularly
important aspect of a Christian church that has Jesus Christ
as its Lord. Without being located where marginalized persons are, a ministry with them is not possible. As Pastor David
Gibbons says, "Greater connection with other communities,
though, comes through our pain, not our successes. Our shame,

marginalization, and invisibility—that is the connection. . . . I found that as I talked in the city, as I shared the pain of my parents' divorce, the interracial issues I worked through, the prejudice I faced, a heart connection happens right away."[20] Gibbons was convinced that his church should be located where the marginalized people are, and persuaded his congregation to relocate the church to a commercially less desirable area of the city. Gibbons wanted his church to be a church of the "misfits" so that it could serve those who are excluded by mainline society as "misfits."[21] Pastor Gibbons knew that the church of Jesus Christ had to be at the periphery.

A few examples of Asian American churches and church members resisting racist practices, working from the peripheries, may be mentioned. The first is the story of Russell Jeung, a professor at San Francisco State University and an evangelical church leader, who, in the 1990s, together with several other Christian laypersons, helped to rectify a terrible owner-neglect situation in Oak Park, a low-income housing development in Oakland, California, occupied by mostly Cambodians and Latinos.[22] Having learned that the poor conditions in the apartment complex were due to an active, calculated neglect by the owner, Jeung moved into the apartment complex to work with the tenants directly on the premises. Soon Jeung was joined by a collection of whites, Latinos, Chinese Americans, and other volunteers, loosely organized as Oak Park Ministries. After working with the tenants to build trust and solidarity among themselves, the group finally filed a lawsuit in 1998. After four years of perseverance, the tenants received $950,000 in damages.

A young Korean American girl was harshly ridiculed and called names by her white schoolmates. The harassment got to the point where the Korean American girl, out of sheer desperation, yelled out, "Stop, or I will kill you!" White students immediately reported to the principal only what the girl said, and she was instantly expelled from the school. About a dozen Korean American lawyers and civic leaders (some of whom were quite possibly church members), went to the principal and explained the desperate circumstances into which this Korean American girl was forced. She was immediately reinstated.

The Church of All Nations in Minneapolis in the early summer of 2009 sponsored a hearing with a panel of community law-enforcement leaders on the practice of police profiling Asian American persons. Many church members spoke to the panel about how they were stopped frequently by the police for no reason at all. A detailed and fact-filled report was subsequently prepared by the panel.

WOMEN AND
THE ASIAN AMERICAN CHURCH

Perhaps the severest critique that I can direct upon Asian American churches has to do with the position of women in many of those churches. In spite of the feminist movement's vigorous and worldwide advocacy of women in recent decades, women are still second-class citizens in many Asian American churches and are not accorded the same respect as men. Many stories are reported of women in Asian immigrant churches being elected as elders or appointed as committee chairs, only to have their male peers meet without their knowledge and make decisions without them.[23]

Peter Cha and Grace May note that recent studies show that the strong ethos of gender hierarchy in the English-speaking congregations are "particularly offensive to second-generation women who are well-educated and have professional careers."[24]

It is not, however, that Asian American women have remained merely as passive victims of the gender oppression in their churches. Sociologist Jung Ha Kim has done an interesting study of Korean American church women in which she found that these women are not mere victims but are active agents who engage in a variety of "subtle and indirect actions" of resistance.[25] Learned silences, quiet refusal to comply with the pastor's unilateral directives, maneuvers behind the scene, and other actions or nonactions, all of which resemble what political scientist James Scott has called the "weapons of the weak," are some of the ways in which Korean American women in churches resist various oppressive powers both within and also outside their ethnic churches.[26]

How does liminality of Asian American women function in their resistance against patriarchy? In chapter 1, I briefly discussed the liminality that women experience when they reject the patriarchal world and leave it behind in search of a new and not-yet-articulated world. Women writers describe this liminality in various ways: "in-betweenness" (Teresa Hak Kyung Cha), "ambiguity and separation" (Penelope Washburn), "nothingness" (Carol Christ), and "awakening" (Inn Sook Lee).[27] Liminality means *communitas*, although it may be experienced covertly and subtly. And in liminality and *communitas*, there is an impetus toward a prophetic stance against the existing order of the society. So just as women experience a double marginalization, they also experience a double liminality/*communitas* (between Asia and America, and between the old patriarchal order of society that women reject and the new order of relationships that they seek). Could we not then expect in women an energy to change the present-day order of society double that in most men? Could we not also say that women have the particular calling, by virtue of their situation, to be the pioneers in the church's work of reforming the patriarchal nature of human living both inside and outside the church?

Women's role as pioneers is amply illustrated by their leadership at crucial times of Jesus' ministry. Mary, the mother of Jesus, had the foresight that in his ministry he was going to "fill the hungry with good things," and send "the rich away empty" (Luke 1:53). The women disciples and followers of Jesus are clearly visible in the Gospel accounts of Jesus' ministry. The Gospel according to Luke mentions Jesus' women "followers": Mary, called Magdalene, Joanna, and Susanna, "and many others who provided for them out of their resources" (Luke 8:1-3). And as New Testament scholar Elisabeth Schüssler Fiorenza points out,

> Just as in the beginning of the Gospel Mark presents four leading male disciples who hear Jesus' call to discipleship, so at the end of the Gospel he presents four leading women disciples and mentions them by name. The four women disciples—Mary of Magdala, Mary, the daughter of wife of James the younger, the mother of Joses, and Salome—were preeminent among the women disciples who have followed Jesus, just as Peter, Andrew, James, and John are preeminent among the twelve.[28]

A Syro-Phoenician woman was a factor in Jesus' widening of his vision for his mission (Matt. 15:21-28). Mary Magdalene anointed Jesus with oil, thus preparing him for his death on the cross while the male disciples had no idea of what she was doing (Luke 7:36-50).

When it comes to the Gospel accounts of Jesus' death on the cross and the resurrection, the role played by Jesus' women disciples and followers was truly remarkable. With the eleven male disciples embarrassingly absent from the scene of the crucifixion, there were women "looking on from a distance . . . and many other women who had come up with him to Jerusalem [from Galilee]" (Mark 15:40-41). According to John's Gospel, "Standing near the cross of Jesus were his mother, and his mother's sister, Mary the wife of Clopas, and Mary Magdalene" (John 19:25). When Joseph of Arimathea laid Jesus' body in a tomb, "the women who had come from Galilee followed, and they saw the tomb and how his body was laid" (Luke 23:55). That was not all. During the night, these women prepared spices and ointments.

After the Sabbath, on the first day of the week, it was Mary Magdalene, according to John's Gospel, who was the first to go to the tomb and find it empty. Not only did she discover the tomb empty, Mary Magdalene was the first to receive a resurrection appearance.

Jesus appeared to her in front of the empty tomb and gave her the commission to "to go to my brothers" and tell them about Jesus' coming ascension (John 20:1, 16-18). Schüssler Fiorenza comments, "Thus in a double sense she becomes the *apostola apostolorum*, the apostle of the apostles," and "thus she is the primary apostolic witness to the resurrection."[29]

Schüssler Fiorenza also makes a more general observation: "Those who are the farthest from the center of religious and political power, the slaves, the children, the gentiles, the women, become the paradigms of true discipleship."[30] Asian American women have as their particular calling to become the paradigms of true discipleship. It is imperative that Asian American churches do not delay in making the necessary changes in their life and work so that their women members may carry out their God-given vocation as pioneers.

MARKS OF THE CHURCH

The Nicene Creed (originally adopted at the Council of Nicaea in 325 but edited into roughly its current form at the Council of Constantinople in 381) states that the church is "one, holy, catholic, and apostolic." The "notes" or "marks" of the church are both descriptive and imperative. Asian American theology must interpret the meaning of these "marks" in its own context.

1. *What is the* one-ness *or* unity *of the Asian American church?* Like churches in other contexts, the Asian American church has its fundamental unity in "one Spirit . . . one faith, one baptism, one God and Father of us all" (Eph. 4:4-6). The church as the "body of Christ" has one head, Jesus Christ the one Lord (1 Corinthians 12).

In actual practice, however, the churches of Jesus Christ are not united. The Protestant church is divided into hundreds of denominations. Closer to home, Korean immigrant congregations, which have served the causes of Christ in so many important ways, have also experienced embarrassingly frequent internal conflicts and divisions.

Whatever the reasons for this divisiveness may be, it has brought to the members of the divided congregations, especially the young people, an untold pain and agony, and is nothing less than a serious scandal. Christian churches across racial and ethnic lines still suffer from lack of unity. In the United States, eleven o'clock on Sunday morning is still the most segregated hour of the week. The unity of the churches, therefore, is not yet a historical reality but a goal to be achieved. This lack of unity, however, does not nullify the ultimate unity of the church rooted in the unity of the three persons of the Trinity. The historical realization of this unity of the church, however, is yet to be actualized.

The particular meaning of the unity of the church for Asian American churches is the unity of the *communitas* of the congregational members that emerges out of their experience of liminality in the worship and life of their churches. In the experiences of *communitas* with God in Jesus Christ, all the differences between persons are neither ignored nor eliminated but embraced and celebrated in a loving communion. Whether the unity of *communitas* is actually being experienced by Asian American churches or not, their liminal predicament is at least then capable of achieving such a unity. This kind of unity as *communitas* could be experienced by the members of different denominations if they meet each other in a liminal space in which they are temporarily freed from as many ecclesial and societal structures as possible.

The unity of *communitas* is actually being experienced across racial and ethnic lines to both small and large degrees in many Asian American churches. Many Asian American churches are finding persons of different racial and ethnic backgrounds joining them both for worship and fellowship. The general commonality of marginalization and liminalization of racial ethnic minority groups in American society, and the use of English in all Asian American churches, may explain, at least partly, the ease with which non-Asian American minority persons join with Asian Americans for their church life.

Consider the case of the Church of All Nations in Minneapolis. This church is "Asian American" only in the sense that its pastor is an Asian American and that it began as an Asian American church. Of its 250 members, 37 percent are white, 20 percent African American, 33 percent Asian American, and 10 percent Latina/o. According to Pastor Jin S. Kim, some white American persons join Asian American churches for two major reasons: first, because those white American Christians are attracted by the lively faith of Asian American churches, and, second, because many of the post-boomers (forty and younger) find all white Caucasian churches "unrealistic" in light of the increasingly diverse nature of American society.[31]

One might ask, Don't the white American members of Asian American churches find the superior power position of white people in America questioned or challenged? One white member of the Church of the All Nations mentioned that any sense of the supremacy of the white people that he might have had in his way of thinking was thoroughly challenged by his minority status in the Asian American congregation and that he felt an acute sense of "self-displacement."[32] Some white persons cannot deal with this challenge and soon leave the Asian American church. Those who end up staying now live with a healthy awareness of the particularity, not superiority, of white people among the many peoples who make up America.

The sense of self-displacement that the white persons in this church experience is an awareness of their liminality. With their sense of liminality, white American persons enter the space of liminality that the racial ethnic minority members of the church already occupy. Out of liminality emerges *communitas*. During my visit to this church I felt an authentic communal fellowship among its people. Liminality was functioning as a means of grace through which the unity of the church was being realized.

2. *The second mark of the church is "holiness."* In ordinary English, the term *holiness* has associations with such concepts as "morality," "sanctity," and "purity." But the most elemental meaning of the

Hebrew word for holiness, *qadhosh*, is "being separated" or "that which is withdrawn from common use."[33] Alister McGrath sees in the original meanings of the term *holy* "strong overtones of dedication: To be 'holy' is to be set apart for and dedicated to the service of God."[34] Following McGrath's interpretation of the term *holy*, the "holiness" of the Asian American church may be seen as its being set apart for the particular vocation of exercising the creative potentials of liminality for God's purposes for creation. As noted earlier, like Galileans in the first century, Asian Americans have the particular vocation of being the "first responders" to Jesus' invitation for people to repent and believe in him. By becoming incarnate as a Galilean and by conducting his ministry primarily in Galilee, God chose to appeal first to the liminal and marginalized Galileans. Galileans were not any better than anyone else. But their liminality made them at least more open to Jesus' message.

Asian Americans are not better than any other group of people. It is, rather, because of Asian Americans' social location of liminality and marginalization that God chose to appeal to them first and hoped that they would be the "first responders." Some women followers fulfilled this vocation of being "first responders" in a remarkable way. A woman was courageously receptive to giving birth to a baby in response to an announcement by God. Women supported materially Jesus' busy ministry. A woman first anointed Jesus preparing him for his death. Women told male disciples of Jesus' resurrection.

Asian American Christians are like the Jewish Christians who lived as exiles in Asia Minor. The author of 1 Peter addresses them as a people "who have been chosen and destined by God the Father and sanctified by the Spirit to be obedient to Jesus Christ" (1:2). The author goes on to declare: "But you are a chosen race, a royal priesthood, a holy nation, God's own people, in order that you may proclaim the mighty acts of him who called you out of darkness into his marvelous light" (2:9). To be chosen by God is "in order that you may proclaim the mighty acts of God." To be chosen, therefore, is not a privilege to boast about. To be set apart by God is always for a purpose. To be chosen is to have a particular vocation and responsibility to carry out. To be so chosen would certainly give a group a sense of cohesion as a group, a sense of belonging, and a sense of purposefulness.[35] To be chosen by God, however, is no reason for pride in oneself.

All Asian Americans, like all Galileans, by virtue of their social location, have been called to the vocation of exercising their liminal creativity for God's purpose in creation. The church, then, is the fellowship of those who respond to this call. The holiness of Asian American churches refers to the fact that they are called and set apart by God for a particular purpose and vocation.

3. *The third mark of the church is "catholicity."* A Christian church is a community of persons who worship the God whose lordship extends to the entire creation. The originating or foundational experience out of which the ecclesial community is born is the experience of God's love and acceptance in Christ that is offered to everyone and anyone who in faith enters into Christ's liminality on the cross. Although the church belongs to a particular culture, nation, or ethnic group or groups, it cannot be limited by boundaries of any kind. All persons are presumed as possible members of a church that is founded upon God's unlimited love. As Edward Farley has put it, the distinctive trait of ecclesia's intersubjective life "derives from the strange way in which the human being who is not a participant in ecclesia is present to those who are participants." "Co-intending strangers," in other words, is "its mode of bonding." And, as Mark Kline Taylor points out, to say that Christian community is marked by the cointending of strangers "is to say that its communal life, ranging from explicit corporate activities to its members' pre-reflective intentions of will, has this feature."[36] Such a posture toward others without boundaries makes a church always decentering, and thus always liminal.[37] The church cannot be catholic without being at the same time liminal.

Fumitaka Matsuoka remarks, "Perhaps the severest critique we can direct upon Asian American churches is that to a certain extent they have been co-opted into the very racist structure of society and thus have come to neglect the most alienated people in society, the poor and the underclass, even among our own Asian Americans."[38] Catholicity of the church, therefore, must begin right where the church is located.

4. *The fourth and final mark of the church is apostolicity.* The fact that the bishops of the church succeed the first apostles cannot be the mark of the essence of the church because what matters about a church cannot be simply the external matter of the apostolic succession of the bishops. What the church is in faith and life would also be essential. Nor should the clergy alone be considered as a part of the essential nature of the church because all members have the calling to follow in their life Jesus Christ, the head of the church. What truly matters must be that the church in faith and life is continuous with the gospel. The church truly succeeds or is faithful to the apostles when the church, in its proclamation and its life, is consistent with the gospel to which the apostles witnessed.

From the perspective of Asian American theology, we recognize in the gospel of Jesus Christ the God who became incarnate as a liminal and marginalized Galilean and appealed first to Galileans because of their liminal openness. The gospel was proclaimed from and embodied in the liminal and peripheral space and not at the center. It was in the space of the extreme liminality of Jesus on the cross that the believers were united with the forgiving and accepting God in Jesus. The church must provide liminal spaces in which the liminal believers can again be united with the loving God in Jesus in Jesus' liminality on the cross.

The gospel of Jesus Christ to which the church must conform is a decentering, countercultural gospel. The gospel is liminal, and those in liminality can approach it. Liminality is the way to the gospel. At the same time, the gospel will lead its believers into liminality, into peripherality. From the perspective of Asian American theology, the gospel is the liminal gospel to which the church must conform. Apostolicity involves liminality. The liminality of the church in its faithfulness to the gospel is its apostolicity.

Chapter 8

THE NEW LIMINALITY AND ASIAN AMERICAN DISCIPLESHIP

After their conversion to the Christian faith, Asian American Christians are still liminal, in-between, and peripheral. Their liminality is now a "new liminality," however. Their liminality is not new in the sense that it is different from their liminality before their conversion to the Christian faith, but in the sense that it is now an intentional liminality that Christians deliberately appropriate as their own.

Asian American Christians choose intentionally the liminal social location or choose to remain in their *de facto* liminal location. They do so because they now belong to the "family of God," the values of which are different from those of the world. Jesus demanded his followers to be totally egalitarian and nonpatriarchal. Jesus asked his disciples to be "poor in spirit" and taught that it was difficult for a rich person to enter the kingdom of God. To follow this Jesus, one must distance oneself from the center of the world and live in liminality, in the periphery. This is why Pastor David Gibbons of the New Song Community Church in Los Angeles realized that to follow Christ inevitably makes one countercultural and asked his people to become a church of the "misfits." Paul makes the point very clearly: "Do not be conformed to this world [or this age], but be transformed by the renewing of your minds, so that you may discern what is the will of God—what is good and acceptable and perfect" (Rom. 12:2).

The transformation that Paul talks about occurs in and through the redeeming *communitas* with God in Christ that the believer experiences as she or he enters the infinite liminality of Jesus on the cross. The Holy Spirit enables the believer to believe and indwells in the believer as she or he strives to live a Christian life. An Asian American Christians' act of distancing himself or herself from the dominant power centers of the world would not be possible without the continuing help of the Holy Spirit.

Asian American Christians who now have a set of values different from the people at the dominant center are already located strategically at the periphery of American culture and society. Peripheral location is now no longer simply *de facto* but intentional and by choice. A question arises: Would it be wrong for an Asian American Christian to achieve a high-ranking and prestigious position within the structure of the dominant center? It would certainly be a good thing for the society as a whole if such a person could be an effective member of the dominant center without sacrificing his or her Christian values. If a person could do that, he or she would be an effective change agent for the dominant group. But it is more likely that it would be highly difficult to follow the rules of the dominant center without compromising one's Christian values. As discussed earlier, the periphery may be the better place from which Christians try to challenge the dominant center and attempt to change it. To be in the world but at its edge is the most strategic posture for Asian American Christians.

So liminality for Asian American Christians after their conversion to Christ is a new liminality, first of all, in that it is now intentional and by choice. Liminality after conversion is new also in the sense that the transforming experience of the *communitas* with Christ on the cross has empowered the Asian American Christian to exercise the creative potentials of his or her liminality in spite of the demoralizing effects of continuing marginalization. There has been a freeing of the suppressed and frustrated potentials of liminality. What Asian American Christians do in exercising their liminal creativity is part of their new existence as Christians. It is their discipleship.

OPENNESS TO THE NEW

What does this exercise of the liminal creativity mean concretely? Consider the examples below.

Lisa Lowe has described the diversity of what constitutes "Asian American" as "heterogeneity, hybridity, multiplicity."[1] To live with an "Asian American" identity is to be open to a variety of cultural and other factors that explicitly or implicitly make up what the term *Asian American* means. Asians are heterogeneous and multiple. Asians have come from the Far East and India, and all the countries in between. The process of critically receiving and rearticulating the cultures from all those nations and cultures without setting some as inferior or superior to others and without exoticizing from the dominant white American perspective is indeed a daunting task. But precisely this is the task facing Asian Americans who would construct an authentic self-identity. One can try to accomplish only a little at a time. But one must by all means be open to them all without giving preference to the familiar or more predominant. Asian American identity must remain porous and open.

The American side of Asian American identity is no less complex. Some racial ethnic minority persons as well as some white Americans think that Americans are white Americans, and American culture is white American culture. Many persons know, of course, that this is not the truth. We Asian American Christians must remember that "American" includes Native Americans, African Americans, Hispanic Americans, and Asian Americans, as well as European Americans. All these peoples and their cultures must figure in Asian Americans' construction of their identity. To do so, Asian Americans must first be open to them and their cultural traditions.

That we must be open to all these peoples is not simply a humanist or commonsense assertion. For us Asian American Christians, our faith demands such an openness. In fact, the Christian faith radicalizes the demand for Asian American Christians' openness to other peoples. What the Christian faith requires of a Christian is an openness to all the peoples in God's world and not just to those who could be categorized as Asians and Americans. The demand is based on the challenge of God's self-revelation in Jesus Christ that those who receive this revelation broaden and open up their remembering. Jesus Christ is the Lord over and in all human history. Therefore, those who are in Christ have entered a lifelong venture of remembering all peoples' history as their history. As H. Richard Niebuhr wrote in *The Meaning of Revelation*:

> [Christ] is the man through whom the whole human history becomes our history. Now there is nothing that is alien to us. All wanderings of all peoples, all the sins of men [*sic*] in all places become parts of our past through him. . . . Through Christ we become immigrants into the empire of God which extends all over the world and learn to remember the history of that empire, that is of men [*sic*] in all times and places, as our history.[2]

Niebuhr, from his christological and radically monotheistic perspective, is giving expression to basically the same point the prophet Jeremiah made out of his conviction regarding God as the creator of all that is. According to Jeremiah, Babylon, where Israelites were taken exiles, is also a land God has made and is under God's rule. Israelites, therefore, should not hesitate to live there and make their home there. Jeremiah writes to the Hebrew exiles:

> Build houses there and live in them; plant gardens and eat what they produce. Take wives and have sons and daughters; take wives for your sons and give your daughters in marriage, that they may bear sons and daughters; multiply there, and do not decrease. But seek the welfare of the city where

> I have sent you into exile, and pray to the LORD on its behalf;
> for in its welfare you will find your welfare. (Jer. 29:5-7)

The circumstances are, of course, different. Israelites in Babylon were exiles; Asian American Christians came to America voluntarily or were born here. But Jeremiah's message applies just the same for Asian Americans. America is part of God's creation. And Asian Americans, as well as all other peoples in America, are God's children. They can all make America their home. Asian American Christians are those who are open to this perspective.

For some first-generation Asian immigrants, it is excruciatingly difficult to cut ties with their homeland and to settle in their newly adopted country. Second- and later-generation Asian Americans sometimes wonder if they are welcome to live in a country that is the only country they have known as their own. To both groups, Jeremiah is saying that America can be your home, because it belongs to God. Niebuhr's quotation above also implies that it is the responsibility and calling of Asian American Christians to consider America their own homeland because Christ is and has been at work in American history as its Lord. Asian American spirituality affirms that America can be our home. We are here to stay. And who is meant here by "we" is open.

COMMUNITAS WITH OTHERS

Communitas with others is a way of relating to others with respect for all their differences, in other words, respect for others in all their otherness. Asian Americans' Christian posture to all others, I would contend, is a readiness to initiate the experience of *communitas* with all others whom they encounter. The "others" here would include the members of the "dominant" group in the United States as well as the "others" who are marginalized by some members of the dominant group.

Some years ago, I had a speaking engagement in Washington, D.C. The flight was seriously late. When I arrived at my hotel, it was past midnight. I was hungry, but the room service was closed. So I went downstairs just to see what I could find for food. The only place that was lit up was the bar, and so I walked in there. The bartender was also leaving, but I saw a lone gentleman sitting on a barstool. The bartender gave me a glass of water. So I sat on a stool next to the gentleman with a drink, and we naturally struck up a conversation.

Here we were out of social structure, in a liminal space. The gentleman told me many things, and finally told me that he was a Vietnam veteran and was torn inwardly about whether or not he would visit the Vietnam War Memorial the next day. He said he wanted to go very badly, but at the same time was deeply afraid to go. He said he did not know how he would respond when he saw his friends' names on the wall. I gently suggested that he should go and that the experience would be good. A few months after I came home, I received a letter from this gentleman who turned out to be a high-ranking executive at a corporation. He wrote that he did go to the memorial, and that the experience was very healing. In liminality, *communitas* had occurred.

I indulge in telling my experiences because they may remind you, the reader, of the *communitas* you have experienced. These *communitas* experiences occur often across racial and ethnic lines, and they could become seeds of alliances, or "solidarity."

And then, there are experiences of momentary, brief experiences of *communitas* with white individuals. I live in a township where most of the residents commute to New York City and are quite accustomed to a great diversity of people. The briefest moments of *communitas* I am speaking about happen usually in the parking lot of a small local shopping mall. This parking lot evidently is a liminal space. Many individual white men and women greet me with a warm smile in the eyes. It's never clear whether I greeted them first, or whether they are positively responding to my silent greeting. At any rate, there is a very brief moment of an expression of goodwill, even delight and pleasure, or what Mark Kline Taylor has aptly called the attitude of "admiration of the other in her, his, or their particular differences."[3] This is, of course, quite a contrast to the long and cold stares I sometimes get when visiting stores farther away from metropolitan areas.

These brief moments of warm greeting, I believe, are the seeds of *communitas*. They are assurances that more full-blown *communitas* is possible. If *communitas* is possible, alliance or solidarity is also possible.

Anselm Kyungsuk Min, in his brilliant book *Solidarity of Others in a Divided World: A Postmodern Theology after Postmodernism*, has eloquently argued that in a world where a great number of diverse people have to live together, the most urgent task is for people to learn to regard others in their otherness and also learn to live and work together in a "solidarity of others." In emphasizing the "solidarity of others," Min is critical of postmodernism's overemphasis on difference. Min writes: "The real issue is not only how each group is going to preserve its otherness and integrity against the ever-present encroachment and domination of an hegemonic group, but also whether and how we as others can and should yet live together by jointly producing those conditions of solidarity that rule out such domination and concretize some sense of the common good."[4] In conceiving the manner of others living together, Min prefers the term *solidarity* to *communion*, because the latter implies, he argues, "a state of union already achieved and an interpersonal, face-to-face relationship." Min continues: "Insofar as all historical relations are always in the dialectical process of change and transcend by far the intimate, interpersonal relations, communion is inadequate and misleading as a historical, social category."[5] I agree with Min that a "larger" category than communion is needed to talk about the alliance of people in the struggle for justice. Solidarity or alliance would be more appropriate. I must also point out, however, that communion in the sense of Victor Turner's *communitas* is not "a state of union" already achieved but, rather, a state of union constantly happening again and again in a dialectical relationship with the condition of liminality.

How is the solidarity of others made possible? Min finds the ultimate model of solidarity with others in the Christian conception of God as the Trinity: "God is a community, a solidarity, of three persons, truly different as persons yet truly united as divine." As the principle of unity in diversity, the Holy Spirit "unites the Father and the Son in their mutual otherness in a communion of Others, and reconciles finite others with the Father by uniting them to the Son in his fellowship with the Father." "The Spirit is active," asserts Min, "wherever there is a movement of self-transcendence toward communion and solidarity on all levels, cosmic, interpersonal, ecclesial, and historical."[6]

How can the others who should be respected in all of their otherness brought together in a relationship of solidarity? Min says that persons must "transcend" themselves in forming solidarity with others, and also that "decentering" of concerns of one's own group is required for solidarity with others.[7]

Min's language is similar to the language of liminality. To "transcend" oneself and to be "decentered" refer to a going beyond a boundary, a structure. To leave one's boundary is to enter into a liminal space. Min's description of the emergence of solidarity is similar to my earlier discussion of the rise of *communitas* out of liminality. The courage to become liminal for the sake of the solidarity of others is another aspect of Asian American spirituality.

RESISTANCE AND THE "HAPPINESS THAT FORGETS NOTHING"

The perspective from a liminal place and the egalitarian ethos of *communitas* both enable the liminal person to raise critical questions about the existing order of human relatedness in the larger society. So liminality and *communitas* encourage liminal persons to resist the unjust aspects of their social existence. Being in Christ gives the believer the courage to stand up against marginalizing forces that oppress human life.

In the previous chapter on the church, I spoke about the prophetic responsibility of Asian American Christians primarily as a group. Here I turn to the prophetic responsibility of Christians as individuals, although the corporate and individual responsibilities are intertwined.

Individual Christians' resistance to the forces of marginalization must begin with themselves. That is to say, there is plenty of marginalizing and dehumanizing going on internally within a human self. The internal oppressive situation must be addressed before a person can effectively resist the oppressive situation in society. Here I would like the reader to indulge some more of my personal introspection.

First, I find myself having to resist an excessive yearning for my homeland in Korea. I spent my childhood and some of my early teen years steeped in nature, as I lived in a small farming town surrounded by creeks and high mountains. After over fifty years in America, I still look for the spring flowers of my hometown, and the sounds of various kinds of cicadas in late summer and fall, and the fall flowers that line the roads. It's probably okay to miss these things. But when I find Korean pine trees far more aesthetically appealing than American pines, then I wonder if I am not clinging too much to the past.

I also wonder at times if I have done the right thing in leaving all the history of my family and ancestors in Korea and transplanting myself in an entirely different culture with a different history and starting a family here away from my roots. Korea will always be my and my descendants' ancestral home. But as generations come and go, this ancestral home will be increasingly no more than a reference point without all the colors, sounds, meanings, and feelings I once knew. Here again, I must resist an overattachment to those roots, and be able to leave home, like Abraham, although I always wonder how Abraham did it.

I must also confess that I probably engage in what can only be called my appeasement of white supremacy. After fifty years of surviving in this country, owing so much to many generous and kind white people, I have attained a habit of mind to try to be overly kind to white people. Partly, my overkindness is a strategy to forestall any rude or mean demeanor from the white American. So whenever I am facing a white American official, serviceperson, business agent, or even sales-person, I tend to become overly obliging and usually address them "Sir," "Ma'am," or "Miss," more than common courtesy requires. (One supermarket meat clerk said to me that I was the first person who called him "Sir" in his entire life.)

Every time I needlessly call somebody "Sir," I say to myself that I must stop doing this. At my age, after half a century in America, I should consider myself equal to anyone as a human being and expect to be treated that way. This internal resistance against my appeasement of white supremacy continues. I have strong survival instincts.

I am also aware of a kind of racist habit I have in relation to the scholars I choose to read. When I look through a list of scholarly writings on the thought of a Western thinker, I tend to think that those articles or books by authors with non-Western names cannot be very good. I probably acquired this habit over the years of living in a Western world that generally is prejudiced in favor of Western scholars over against the non-Western, especially when the subject matter is Western in content. For some years now I deliberately try to resist this prejudice when I look over a bibliography on a Western thinker.

The Christian spirituality of resistance cannot be limited to the resistance against racism and racial and ethnic prejudice. A recent book entitled *Resistance: The New Role of Progressive Christians*, edited by John B. Cobb Jr., lists five "dominant forces" in America today that Christians are called to resist: consumerism, poisonous inequality, American imperialism, scientism, and global warming.[8] The small steps that individual Christians can take in promoting countercultural values are where we must begin.

The spirituality of the new liminality and *communitas* cannot be limited to prophetic resistance. It also celebrates the reign of God that is already here and now. Asian American spirituality includes happiness and joy. Mexican American theologian Virgilio Elizondo points out that "the prophetic without the festive turns into cynicism and bitterness, or simply fades away."[9] But happiness and joy for Asian American spirituality are happiness and joy "that forget nothing"—that is, are fully aware of the difficulties and problems facing Asian Americans (more on this below).

The words *happiness* and *joy* need a brief comment. The Greek word that is translated as "blessed" in the Beatitudes in the Gospels is *makarios,* which means "fortunate," "happy," "in a privileged situation," "well-off."[10] The meaning of the English term *happiness* is wide ranging: gladness, feeling fortunate, contentment, tranquility, blessedness, in union with God, and so on.[11] Jonathan Edwards considered happiness as a state that combines both the knowledge of true beauty and the delight in and love of true beauty.[12] Joy is too ecstatic. Happiness seems to be a broader term than "joy," referring to a basic affection of the entire person who is in harmony with his life and with the ultimate reality.

The basic affection of happiness in Asian American spirituality is rooted in our knowledge that God has won the decisive victory over evil and that we live with the expectation of the complete actualization of that victory in all areas of God's creation. Asian Americans' life in America, in spite of all the difficulties, is not without the benefit of God's gracious blessings, for which we should be grateful and happy. I came to this country with $150 in my pocket over fifty years ago, and for all that time, I have not gone hungry even for one day. America to many people is a land of opportunity, and its people are generous. I am not forgetting that this "generosity" is often condescending and patronizing. But I am simply admitting that without such generosity, I might not have survived. There also have been individuals whose support, friendship, and generosity have been a pure embodiment of God's grace. Happiness to a significant extent is gratitude.

Once I was flying back from Seoul, South Korea, after one of my many trips to my homeland. As the plane was approaching John F.

Kennedy Airport, I was again troubled by the contradictory character of my feelings. I felt good that I was coming home, to my family and to my house. At the same time, I was asking myself, "Why am I coming to a foreign country again?" To have both of these feelings was somewhat troubling. I was coming to my home in America, but America still was not my home.

Soon I was lined up with my baggage for customs inspection. One white American customs officer was sitting on a stool quickly glancing at everyone's customs report form. He let some go on out to the arriving area and asked others to remain for some further inspection. My turn came, and he looked at my passport and said I could go. But as he let me go, he looked at me and said, " Mr. Lee, welcome home!" What he said literally overwhelmed me. As I was walking to the door to the arrival area, I noticed that my eyes were tearing up a little and I still think, years later, that I should have gone back and thanked him for saying what he said.

Now I need to say a word about the phrase I mentioned earlier, "the happiness that forgot nothing," which comes from Albert Camus's novel *The Plague*. For Camus, being aware of the reality of human life, however ambiguous or often painful it may be, is a fundamental requirement for an authentic existence. So even "happiness," which Camus once defined as "the simple harmony between a man [*sic*] and the life he leads," has to be "the happiness that forgot nothing, not even murder."[13]

Miroslav Volf, in his brilliant and profound book *Exclusion and Embrace: A Theological Exploration of Identity, Otherness, and Reconciliation*, presents a very different view of remembering and forgetting. According to Volf, exclusion suffered in the past is still an exclusion if it is not forgotten. If we remember suffering and injustice of the past, we will never "be whole." If we remember the pain of the past, suffering will never stop, and we will only end up with "an unredeemed sadness." Volf argues that since redemption includes the redemption of the past, and since the pain and injustices of the past cannot be dissolved through theodicies, only forgetting or nonremembering can help. "Put starkly," says Volf, "the alternative is: either heaven or the memory of horror. . . . Redemption will be complete only when the creation of 'all things new' is coupled with the passage of 'all things old' into the double *nihil* of non-existence and non-remembrance."[14]

My main objection to Volf's point of view is that if pain and injustices are forgotten, then their seriousness is not duly recognized and respected. Just to forget is too easy an answer on matters as grave as exclusion and dehumanization. It is a too easy way out, it seems. My conception of heaven is not where all bad things are forgotten, but where all tragic and painful things are fully remembered yet they do not shatter us the way they used to. Heaven is where all the injustices are remembered and also rectified. What do we do, on this side of heaven, with the wounds and pain that we remember? After a while, are we not often granted the power to live with our wounds and pain rather than being overwhelmed by them? Are we not granted the power to carry our crosses on our shoulders rather than be carried by them?

Memories of wounds and pain can also lead to healing. Jesus' resurrected body bore the wounds of the cross, and those wounds helped Jesus himself and doubting Thomas remember the crucifixion and restored Thomas's relationship with his Lord. Pilgrimages to the sites of the Japanese American internment during World War II help the victims and others to remember the suffering and thereby help them begin the process of coming to terms with it and of being healed.[15] I would side with Camus and insist that true happiness forgets nothing.

As a prototype of the celebrative happiness of Asian American discipleship, I think of the breakfast that the resurrected Jesus prepared for his disciples by the Sea of Galilee (John 21:1-14). Jesus surprised the disciples by appearing on the beach early in the morning. He helped them catch a large amount of fish. Jesus then prepared a charcoal fire to cook some of the fish they caught. The disciples were still not completely sure who this visitor was. Jesus then invited them, "Come and have breakfast." Though marginalized and liminal as a region, Galilee still has beautiful beaches where friends can have breakfast by the sea. We must imagine Jesus happy and not forgetting anything in front of the charcoal fire.

Chapter 9

LIMINALITY AND RECONCILIATION

THE TASK OF RECONCILIATION

Fumitaka Matsuoka argues in his book *The Color of Faith* that conversation across racial differences has become so difficult that we are gradually reduced to silence. "Where there is a loss of conversation, human life withers and dies," writes Matsuoka. He is also firmly convinced that only a reconciliation between peoples under the power of the gospel of forgiveness and love can break down the walls of hostility, and get people talking to each other again.[1]

Reconciliation is indeed at the heart of the gospel. The God of the Christian faith demands of human beings more than a mere coexistence. The very purpose for which God created the world was to repeat the inner-trinitarian communion in time and space. Human life, therefore, has an ultimate meaning only as it gets caught up in the divine energy toward the communion of human beings with God and among themselves. Asian American Christians, therefore, by virtue of their communion with the triune God incarnated in Christ, have as their vocation to work toward a reconciliation and a communion of all persons, including those who marginalize and oppress others.

Reconciliation, however, especially from the perspective of the oppressed victims, is a difficult proposition. James H. Cone, speaking from the African American context, passionately argues in his book *God of the Oppressed* that liberation is the precondition of reconciliation. Cone's insistence on the priority of liberation stems from his theological presupposition that God's redemptive act in history was an event of liberation, liberation in the political, economic, and social sense. At the same time, however, Cone draws from the practical experiences of African Americans in the United States. Cone was writing at the time when African Americans were becoming acutely aware of the fact that white people's talk of "integration" really meant an integration on white people's terms. He insists that there first has to be a fundamental change in the power relations between whites and blacks. He writes: "We must let them know that there can be no communication between masters and slaves until the *status* of master no longer exists." Cone continues, "A word about reconciliation too soon or at the wrong time to the oppressors only grants them more power to oppress black people."[2]

Other theologians have suggested a more realistic view of what can be realized on this side of the eschaton. Miroslav Volf points out that what Christians can achieve in this history is imperfect and penultimate when compared with the perfect reconciliation to be actualized in the New Heaven and New Earth. What can be achieved in this life is "a nonfinal reconciliation based on a vision of reconciliation that cannot be undone." "The final reconciliation," says Volf, is the backdrop against which Christians engage in the struggle for peace under the condition of enmity and oppression."[3] John de Gruchy also finds it necessary to make a distinction between the "language of the penultimate and that of the ultimate, between the secondary and primary expressions of reconciliation." Reconciliation in the second sense, according to de Gruchy, "is work in progress, a dynamic set of processes into which we are drawn and in which we participate."[4]

Miroslav Volf also points out that an eschatological perspective is needed in regard to the notion of justice. Justice has to be universal. God's justice is, of course, universal. Human ideas of God's justice,

however, are not universal. Human reason cannot help justice overcome the particularity, Volf points out, "because unable to survive sus-
pended in mid-air, it always situates justice within a particular vision
of the good life." He continues, "Unable to transcend particularities,
justice must continue to struggle against justice."[5] Our account of justice cannot be universal.

In discerning what is just, a Christian therefore must practice
what Volf calls a "double vision," a seeing "with the eyes of the others, accepting their perspective, and discovering the new significance
of one's own commitments." Volf explains further: "We need to see
our judgment about justice and struggle against injustice through the
eyes of the other—even the manifestly 'unjust other'—and be willing
to readjust our understanding of justice and repent of acts of injustice." In order to practice this "double vision," one must care about
the other as other. In other words, Volf says, "There can be no justice
without the will to embrace."[6] Love, in other words, shapes the very
content of justice. Volf says, "true justice will always be on the way to
embrace." Using the theological terms of Jonathan Edwards, we can
say that since God's ultimate end in creation is loving communion, justice is true justice only when it serves loving communion. To discern
justice with love for the other is to realize that one's notion of justice is
always provisional.

A Christian's realization of the provisional character of the historically achievable reconciliation and justice, however, should not
dampen his or her commitment to work for reconciliation and justice.
The eschatological qualification should free Christians from being dis-
illusioned by the imperfections of reconciliation and justice that they
do achieve. They should also be encouraged in their work for reconciliation and justice by the knowledge that the ultimate realization of
reconciliation and justice is promised in the future and will be brought
about by God Godself.

I return here for a moment to James Cone's insistence that liberation or the establishment of justice must precede reconciliation.

Although I may not agree with Cone that one must "precede" the other, I certainly agree with the spirit of his assertion: namely, reconciliation and work for justice must go together. As John Calvin insisted, "Christ justifies no one whom he does not sanctify at the same time."[7] If an African American and a white American shook each other's hands over a racist act by the white person, and if the white person did absolutely nothing actually to change his or her racist attitude and the racist nature of American culture, such a handshake could not in any way be thought of as an act of reconciliation. If the handshake were called an act of reconciliation, it would be empty of any meaning. Reconciliation and work for justice cannot be separated from each other.

THE ROLE OF LIMINALITY IN RECONCILIATION

Reconciliation is a restoration of human relationship, and liminality is the condition out of which communion between human beings emerges. Liminality, therefore, can lead to reconciliation. Ultimately, human reconciliation is the work of the Holy Spirit as the mutual love between the Father and the Son. But liminality can function as a means of grace, as an instrument that the Holy Spirit uses. Liminality may indeed be a necessary facilitator of reconciliation, although it cannot be a sufficient facilitator.

Miroslav Volf identifies four essential elements in the movement from exclusion to embrace: repentance, forgiveness, making space in oneself for the other, and healing of memory. What Volf describes as "making room in oneself for the other" seems very similar to what I mean by liminality. The process of reconciliation or embrace moves on beyond forgiveness to the stage of making room in oneself even for one's enemies. In doing so, Volf explains, we imitate the triune God who in the agony on the cross lets there be an opening or "fissure" through which estranged humanity can come in and join the divine dance of the triune communion. God's love that "sustains non-self-enclosed identities in the Trinity seeks to make space 'in God' for humanity." And, "having been embraced by God, we must make space for others in ourselves and invite them in—even our enemies," writes Volf.[8]

After discussing the four elements in the movement from exclusion to embrace, Volf turns to the story of the prodigal son in the New Testament (Luke 15:11-32), which he interprets as a "drama of embrace" consisting of four acts. In his discussion, Volf explains further what is meant by "making room in oneself." Act I of the drama is the opening of the arms. "Open arms," says Volf, are "a sign that I have created space in myself for the other to come in." Volf describes the meaning of the self's "making room in itself" as "withdraw[ing] from itself . . . away from the limits of its own boundaries," and also creating "a fissure in oneself" or "an aperture on the boundary of the self through which the other can come in."[9]

Act II is "waiting." Volf explains, "after creating space in itself and coming out of itself, the self has 'postponed' desire and halted at the boundary of the other." Volf continues: "We can describe waiting as the work of desiring self on itself for the integrity of the other—the other who may not want to be embraced but left alone."[10] Act III is "closing the arms." This part of the embrace is reciprocal. "In an embrace a host is guest and guest is a host," explains Volf. Volf also insists that "In an embrace the identity of the self is both preserved and transformed, and the alterity of the other affirmed as alterity and partly received into the ever changing identity of the self."[11] Act IV is "opening." The opening of the arms signifies that the integrity of the other as outer must be preserved, and merging of both into an undifferentiated "we" must be avoided. The open arms of the fourth act are the same open arms of the first act in which the self made a room for the other and desired the other's presence. The open arms in the fourth act also open up the boundary of the self and issue an invitation for the other to return.

All of Volf's descriptions of the meaning of "the self's making room in itself," as indicated earlier, leave the impression that what Volf has in mind here is very similar to what I mean by "liminality" or "liminal space," which one enters by leaving behind structures and boundaries. The embracing self goes beyond the boundaries of the self, makes an opening for the other, and thereby enters a liminal space. In this liminal space, the embracing self and the embraced self meet, and there emerge *communitas* and reconciliation.

After his discussion of the steps taken in the act of embrace, Volf engages in a brilliant analysis of the parable of the prodigal son, as an illustration of what goes into the act of embrace. Volf concludes his analysis by stating that "guided by the indestructible love which makes space in the self for others in their alterity, which invites the others who have transgressed to return, which creates hospitable conditions for their confession, and rejoices over their presence, the father keeps re-configuring the order without destroying it so as to maintain it as an order of embrace rather than exclusion."[12]

I suggest that a close reading of the text reveals an even greater role of liminality in the prodigal son's story than Volf notices. The text includes the following words: "But while he [the returning son] was still far off, his father saw him and was filled with compassion; he ran and put his arms around him and kissed him" (Luke 15:20). The important words are: "he [the father] ran." In traditional Jewish culture, as in Asian, fathers do not run to greet their children. The father waits in his room while the son greets his mother and other members of the family. Only then does the son respectfully walk into his father's room and greet him. It has also been pointed out to me that when a Jewish father runs, his ankles would be exposed bare, and that any respectable father would not let this happen. So the prodigal son's father, moved by his compassion for his son, ends up acting in such a way that takes him out of his social structure, role, and status. He enters a liminal space, in which he is freed from the social order and mores that were his boundaries. The prodigal son is already in a liminal condition. The son confesses that he has sinned and that he is not worthy to be with his father. The son meets his father with no status in his house and family and thus in the social structure. In this liminal space, the father and the delinquent son meet, and *communitas* and reconciliation happen. The story repeats the story of how God in Christ entered an extreme liminal space on the cross, and how in that space redeeming communion between God in Christ and sinners happens.

Two cases illustrate well how liminality plays a key role in bringing about reconciliation and communion. The first has to do with a multicultural-multiethnic church in a midwestern city and the other with the pilgrimages conducted to the sites of the Japanese Americans' internment during World War II.

The Church of All Nations in Minneapolis, mentioned earlier, began as a Korean American church with senior pastor Jin S. Kim, himself a Korean American, as the founding pastor. Now, white Americans are the congregation's fastest-growing group.

Pastor Kim knew from the start that if one group played a dominant and normative role, then the church would not really be multicultural or multiethnic. So he strongly challenged the two largest groups, the white Americans and Asian Americans, to give up any ideas of their supremacy and normativity in the church's life and work. Pastor Kim's idea was that each and every group should think of itself as a particular group, with no one claiming to be the dominant group.

This challenge from the pastor hit the white American members especially hard because they were accustomed to being the "normative" Americans in U.S. society. White American members were being asked to stop thinking in terms of "white supremacy," because of which all racial and ethnic minority people in this country have been marginalized for a long time. The pastor challenged the white members of the church to give up their very identity as the dominant group both in the church and in the society at large.

During one weekend in November, 2009, I flew to Minneapolis and visited the church. After the Sunday morning service, I interviewed several white American members of the church and asked them how the pastor's challenge affected them. A few of them mentioned the word *displacement*. They felt they were "displaced" from their normative and superior status in American society. What they were used to assuming in American culture the people at the church now questioned. In this way, a white person is thrown into a no-man's land where his or her identity is going to have to be reconstructed. White persons are thrown into the liminal space. A very sensitive white person whom I interviewed talked about the pain that accompanies his feeling of displacement and his reexamination of his identity.

The liminal space, however painful and disorienting it may be at times, is a creative space from which new identities may emerge and also *communitas* may be formed. Through a phone conversation that I conducted sometime after my visit to the church, the same white person whom I had interviewed before said to me, "I was displaced but also more *deeply placed*—more deeply placed into my particularity. I was now placed beyond my whiteness into my particular ethnic background."[13] He went on to say that the experience of displacement was liberating and made him more open, and that this kind of openness led to community with others.

The liminal space opened up by displacement functioned as a liberating space in which a white person's authentic and particular (not universal and dominant) self-identity (such as Italian American, English American, French American, etc.) could be owned for the first time and a new communal relationship based on equality with others could be formed. The person on the phone also said, "There are so many layers in the whiteness in American culture, and I am having to deal with them one at a time. It is an ongoing process." This church has put this young man on a sometimes painful and disorienting but ultimately liberating journey toward his authentic self.

It is not possible to tell, of course, how many of the white church members go through painstaking introspective reflection about the meaning of a white person's identity. But there is no question that the entire church is aware of the pastor's demand that everyone who joins this church is choosing to be "a minority" and to " 'lay down the sword' of power and privilege." One white American intern at the church expressed it this way: "Multicultural means submission. Even though you don't want to give up [your own way], you do, because you love your brother."[14]

So white Americans become liminal when they come to this church. The nonwhite members of the church were already marginalized and liminal before they joined the church, and this multicultural and multiethnic church provides them with a safe place to be aware of their minority status and their liminality. Out of liminality emerges *communitas*. In the Church of All Nations, I had a genuine impression that everyone there had a sense of belonging to each other. Pastor Jin Kim says, "In this church, there is more community than any of the members' preexisting social networks."[15]

Before the Sunday morning worship, people in the pews talked softly to each other. Some got up from their seats and went over to their friends to chat. The talk was subdued. But the conversation was not the sort of empty talk that people sometimes engage in before a worship service. The conversations all seemed serious and about some concrete and important matters. The talk was a family talk. It was conversation among the best of friends. This family talk went on until just before the service. It was a most interesting and moving sight to observe. This was a reconciled people—or, at least, friends on the way to reconciliation.

The complexity of the issues of justice and reconciliation is nowhere more apparent than in the case of the U.S. internment of Japanese American residents and citizens during World War II. In the midst of the hysteria created by the Japanese attack on Pearl Harbor on December 7, 1941, the U.S. government, under Executive Order 9066, blatantly violated the Constitution by forcibly evacuating 120,000 Japanese residents and American-born Japanese American citizens out of their homes and businesses and by imprisoning them in hurriedly constructed so-called relocation centers located in uninhabited, desolate areas of several western states.

The magnitude and depth of the pain and shame that this "concentration camp" experience inflicted upon the internees will probably never be completely understood. The Japanese American internment experience is complex especially because of the reluctance of the Issei and Nisei (the first and second generation) internees to talk about their camp experiences. Their silence has frustrated and in some cases alienated Sansei (third generation) Japanese Americans. Some have appealed to the Japanese cultural concept of shame as the reason for the internees' "silence." But their silence may also be their way of communicating the unspeakable nature of their pain and shame.

In face of this complex reality of the interment and its aftermath, one very healing and constructive activity has been the pilgrimages that have been conducted to former campsites. This project originated in 1969 when students from the University of California at Davis organized the first pilgrimage to the former internment campsite in Newell, California, near the Oregon border, bringing together students, community activists, and former internees.

Pilgrims leave their homes and the structure of their social existence and join the fellow pilgrims in a transitional, in-between space of the journey. By being placed in such a liminal space, the pilgrims can be expected to experience an openness to ideas and realities to which they had not been open before, an emergence of *communitas* among them, and the motivation to try to effect an change when they return to structure. Joanne Doi, a theologian and Asian American studies scholar, has led the pilgrimages and has done a careful study of the pilgrimage to Tule Lake, California.

The in-between or liminal nature of pilgrimage, according to Doi, provides the Japanese American participants an opportunity to become self-consciously aware of the liminal nature of their existence in American society and to embrace it for what it is without trying to resolve, solve, or transcend it. In the openness and freedom of liminality, there occurs a kind of reconciliation between Japanese American pilgrims and the truth of their liminal predicament in the United States. The reconciliation is between the self that does not wish to face up to the ambiguous reality of liminality and the self that knows the truth.

The liminality of the pilgrimage gives rise to *communitas* which, according to Doi, includes a "communion with the dead."[16] In liminality, which is like the state of timelessness inhabited by the dead, the pilgrims hear the dead, and the stories of the dead become the pilgrims' own stories. Or, put differently, the stories of the dead and their suffering help the pilgrims in weaving their own life stories into some meaningful whole. In liminality, the pilgrims learn to live with the whole tragedy of internment by owning it as a part of the stories of their own lives. This is yet another kind of reconciliation that occurs in the liminality of the pilgrimage.

So liminality facilitates reconciliation and communion among persons. Asian Americans can utilize their liminality to work for reconciliation and communion. Asian American Christians by virtue of their faith have as their particular responsibility to use their liminality to participate in God's own work of repeating in this world God's own inner-trinitarian communion.

Chapter 10

A NEW HEAVEN AND
A NEW EARTH

The Christian hope in the ultimate realization of the reign of God and of God's complete victory over all the forces that oppose God is based on God's decisive victory over sin and evil, and God's inauguration of a new existence for the fallen creation through the resurrection of the crucified Jesus. To put the matter in terms of the doctrine of creation, the Christian faith in the ultimate actualization of what God intended for humanity and for the whole creation is rooted in the faithfulness and power of God in accomplishing the end for which God originally created the world. The biblical witness uses a number of symbols (including "heaven," "a new heaven and a new earth") to refer to the state of creation in which God is "all in all" (Rev. 4:10; 21:1; 1 Cor. 15:28). In articulating a brief eschatology in Asian American context, I make use of two basic ideas (the progressive nature of heaven and Christ's continuing mediating role in heaven) in the eschatology of colonial American theologian Jonathan Edwards.

In terms of what we know as human beings, one wonders if there is any hope for the future of humanity and of the universe. As a marginalized racial minority, many Asian Americans wonder whether racism will ever be eradicated from human societies. Some scientists speak about the gradual entropy of the universe. But the Christian hope in the future of the created world is not based on any scientific knowledge, nor is the realization of this hope thought to be based on human abilities and efforts. The Christian hope is grounded in the Hebrew people's and Christians' experience of the faithfulness of God who is the creator of life itself. Only God's creative action, not human striving, can bring about the realization of God's own purpose for the creation. This, however, does not mean that human beings have no role to play in the realization of God's will on earth. God, rather, works in and through human efforts. Human striving, therefore, by God's grace can participate in what God is doing to bring about God's reign.

What is the nature of heaven or "the new heaven and the new earth"? As Jonathan Edwards would say, heaven is a dynamic and "progressive" state.[1] As noted earlier, the end for which God created the world is to repeat God's inner-trinitarian beauty and communion *ad extra*, that is, in time and space. Since the beauty of God's loving communion *ad intra* is infinite, and temporality and space and the human beings who live in time and space finite (i.e., of a limited capacity), it will take an everlasting time for God's end in creation to be accomplished fully. As Edwards notes, the point in time will never come when God's project of repeating God's internal glory in finite time is ever completed.

Therefore, the history of fallen humanity will come to an end at the eschaton, the last day of *this* history. But history as such will continue in a new heaven and a new earth. The history of God's redemption of fallen humanity will come to an end. But the history of God's repetition of God's internal beauty in time and space will continue. The degree of the actualization of God's project to repeat God's internal glory in time and space will become closer and closer to the infinite degree but will never come to an identity with God's internal glory itself.[2]

It is not that one event of the repetition of God's internal loving communion in time and space through the sanctified Christians' loving communion with God through Christ is not a *true and real* repetition of God's internal glory. It is, rather, that God's internal glory is infinite, and human capacity only finite, that it will take a never-ending and ever-increasing repetition of God's glory in time to realize God's end in creation. Therefore, new repetitions of God's glory in time and space must be "added" to the earlier ones, so that there will be an ever-increasing repetition of God's glory in time and space. God's essential nature is God's eternal disposition to actualize God's inner loving communion both *ad intra* and *ad extra*.[3] God's repeated exercises of God's disposition is what underlies the everlasting repetition of God's glory in heaven.

The sanctified persons in heaven are happy in their participation in God's loving communion in time and space. But this happiness is not a state of a satiated and dull happiness. The believers' happiness in heaven is, rather, a true and satisfied happiness that at the same time has a joyous hope for future additions of more happiness as they look toward the future repetitions of God's loving communion. Their hope is not an anxious and apprehensive hope but a joyous hope because there is a certainty that those future additions to happiness will occur.

As the biblical symbol "a new heaven and a new earth" indicates, the physical dimension of the creation, including the bodies of human beings, is included in heaven. Human beings see with their eyes, and hear with their ears, except that their capacities are drastically improved.[4]

The incarnation of the second person of the Trinity continues. Jesus Christ with his human body continues in heaven the work of mediating human beings' experience of the redeeming *communitas* with the gracious God in Jesus Christ. In heaven liminality continues to exist, although marginalization no longer occurs. The liminality of Jesus Christ in heaven consists of emptying himself of his status as the second person of the Trinity and assuming a humble human form. In this sense, Jesus Christ stands outside of his structure in meeting human beings. Those who would follow Jesus also meet him in his liminal space through their own liminality. Whatever structure human beings may have in heaven, they leave that structure behind in meeting with Jesus. Out of their meeting with Jesus in this liminal space, a loving *communitas* experience occurs. In and through this *communitas* experience with Jesus Christ the believers experience the gracious and loving God, the Father of Jesus Christ. This experience of a loving communion with God in Jesus Christ happens again and again. Each time, communion with God becomes more and more intimate.

This loving communion, of course, includes the believers' perception of the beauty of God as a God of loving communion. The emphasis here is on the believers' being accepted into God's loving communion rather than the medieval notion of "seeing God" (beatific vision), although, as noted above, entering into a loving communion with God includes the "seeing" of God's beauty as the God of loving communion.

In this way, Jesus Christ continues in heaven his role of mediating the communion with the transcendent God for finite humanity.[5] The continued incarnation of the second person of the Trinity and his mediating work is necessary because God's end for creation is the ever-increasing repetition of God's inner-trinitarian communion in and through the human believers' loving communion with God and their neighbors.

The believing human beings' communion with God in Jesus Christ is the primary reality in heaven, but they also have other relationships that are not directly a relationship with God. Theologian Daniel L. Migliore points out that heaven must be a place where society and institutions also exist in their perfected form.[6] Human society and institutions will continually be engaged in a dialectic between *communitas* and structure. Those persons who belong to them must meet each other in liminal spaces and experience *communitas*. And when they return to the structure of the groups, those who return continually help imbue those groups with a loving communal spirit. So the inhabitants of heaven will have *communitas* experiences that are not directly a *communitas* experience of God. But the loving communal spirit of believers' *communitas* with God would pervade the ethos of all groups and communities in heaven, so that God is indeed "all in all" (1 Cor. 15:28). In the fallen world, the spirit of *communitas* is never completely taken into the structure. But in heaven, structure is completely imbued with the communal and egalitarian spirit of *communitas*.

The particularity of human and social existence would not be abolished in heaven. The unity that prevails there will not be a static uniformity but a communal unity that embraces particularity. The author of the book of Revelation writes that in heaven "there was a great multitude that no one could count, from every nation, from all tribes and peoples and languages, standing before the throne and before the Lamb, robed in white, with palm branches in their hands" (Rev. 7:9). Particular "peoples" and "languages" will exist in heaven. But there is no hierarchy whereby certain peoples are nobler than others and certain languages more universal than others. All stand before "the Lamb" as equal beneficiaries of God's forgiving grace.

In the fallen world, some groups of people believe that they are superior to others and that what they think and believe should be the standard for all people. They believe they are "universal" and forget their "particularity." Theologian Benjamin Reist expresses his hope that the white population in the United States will realize their particularity, as follows:

> And the road to inexhaustible freedom for whites involves becoming neither black nor red, but white, for the first time. It involves becoming white as liberated into particularity, the particularity of being one component in the full mosaic that is humanity; becoming white in such a way that white cannot be white unless red and black are equally present in the historical space that is human liberation.[7]

Particularity, of course, should not be absolutized. Some unity that preserves particularity must be achieved if all particulars are going to flourish. The point is that no particular be allowed to establish itself as the hegemonic, the universal.

The element of continuity in what God accomplishes through sanctified persons in heaven and this world makes what happens in human history here on earth a matter of ultimate importance. In some theological perspectives, heaven and this world are dualistically conceived in such a way that what happens in this world is ultimately not important in contrast to what happens in the "really real" world of heaven. In such a dualistic perspective, human suffering in this world is not taken with an ultimate seriousness and is sometimes regarded as worthwhile trials that will be compensated by great blessings in heaven. Today, many thinkers, theological and otherwise, reject this kind of belittling of this-worldly existence. One of the main characters in Albert Camus's novel *The Plague*, after watching all night the torturous suffering to which a plague-stricken child is subjected, is moved to ask, "For who would dare to assert that eternal happiness can compensate a single moment's human suffering?"[8]

The vision of the everlasting life outlined in this chapter does not belittle this-worldly life here on earth in time and space. This is so because God's repetitions of God's internal communion in and through the human communion with God in Jesus Christ here on earth are in the same series with such repetitions in heaven. God's repetitions of God's internal communion in this history count toward the totality of such repetitions that will finally accomplish the end for which God created the world. Every formation of loving communion with God in Jesus and with other human beings and also the physical universe in this history, just as much as such formations in heaven, counts toward the accomplishment of God's project of enlarging God's beauty *ad extra*.

The Christian hope for "the new heaven and the new earth," therefore, can never be an excuse for being indifferent to suffering and injustice in this life here and now. On the contrary, the hope for future fulfillment should function as the basis for a greater incentive to struggle against injustice and to alleviate suffering. As theologian Jürgen Moltmann puts it, "Those who hope in Christ can no longer put up with reality as it is. . . , for the goal of the promised future stabs inexorably into the flesh of every unfulfilled present."[9]

CONCLUSION

Following Jesus Christ involves being located at the periphery or the liminal place and not at the center of society. One cannot be open to the values of the reign of God if one is caught up in the structure of the dominant center. One cannot relate to the alienated of the society if one is not ready to meet them at a liminal place. One cannot be a prophetic voice against the dominant center if one is a part of the structure of that center. And if to be located at the periphery instead of the dominant center is an essential requirement for following Christ, to be so located is then the requirement for all Christians and not only for Asian American Christians.

It is, however, not an easy thing for a white person to detach herself or himself from the culture of the center. White persons experience the pain of dislocation as they try to think of themselves no longer as the norm but as simply one of many people who live in a diverse and multicultural society. White persons who locate themselves at the periphery also risk being rejected by their own people who are at the dominant center. Since white persons live in a society where they make up the dominant center, it is so easy for them to return to that center. White Christians must constantly resist the temptation to turn away from the periphery. To follow Christ is definitely a way of the cross.

Asian American Christians have the calling to be located at the periphery. But in two important ways their task is different from that of white American Christians. First, Asian Americans are already at the periphery. As Christians, they are called not just to remain at the periphery, but also to choose to remain there with a new purpose and a new perspective. In choosing to remain at the periphery, there is the danger of romanticizing the periphery as an inherently good location. The periphery in itself is not a more desirable place over other places. Christians are called to be at the periphery because it is a strategic location. It is strategic place for open-mindedness, *communitas*, and prophetic voice vis-à-vis the center.

Asian American Christians' calling to be at the periphery is also different from the white Christians' vocation to be so located in that Asian Americans are marginalized and thus pushed to be the periphery. Asian Americans, with a few exceptions, are denied complete social acceptance by the people at the center and are excluded from the privilege to pursue their happiness at the cultural, political, and social center of American society. To be pushed to the periphery, for Asian Americans, means to be demoralized, humiliated, and dehumanized.

What does it mean to demand that Asian American Christians remain at the place to which their marginalization has pushed them?

Periphery is both the place to which marginalization pushes Asian American Christians, and also a liminal place with its creative potentials. Christians are those who have the moral strength to exercise the creative potentials of liminality in spite of marginalization. Asian American Christians are called to claim the periphery as a liminal space and resist the marginalization that would push them to the periphery.

What Asian American Christians resist cannot be their location at the periphery as such but, rather, the racist exclusion by the white dominant center that forces them to the periphery. Further, the goal of Asian American Christians' resistance cannot be to overthrow white people's dominance and to establish Asian American dominance. Asian

American Christians then would become just the same as what they are resisting.

For Asian American Christians, their peripheral location is also a liminal space. And the marginalization of Asian Americans constantly threatens to turn periphery into a place of demoralization. But Asian American Christians now have the moral strength to exercise the creative potentials of liminality in spite of marginalization. *Communitas* will emerge from their liminality and help them withstand the demoralizing consequences of marginalization. In this struggle for *communitas* and against marginalization, Asian American Christians can be pioneers. The exercise of liminal creativity for the values of the reign of God is a special vocation of Asian American Christians because their very life in America is *de facto* in a liminal and marginalized context. One may hope that many Asian American Christians will become self-consciously liminal, will exercise their liminal creativity to promote God's end in creation, and will encourage white Americans to enter their own liminal spaces and experience the *communitas* of Christ. When all peoples face up to their liminal spaces, the *communitas* of Christ, and not the dominant centers, will prevail. Asian American Christians can encourage others to enter their own liminal spaces at the periphery and live in the *communitas* of Christ.

In line with God's end in creating the world, Asian Americans' purpose in resisting the dominant center can only be *communitas*, the loving community with white people and with all other peoples. *Communitas*, along with reconciliation with those who marginalize us, is the only legitimate Christian purpose for resisting the dominant center. The goal is to meet all others in liminal spaces and establish *communitas*.

NOTES

CHAPTER 1

1. Everett V. Stonequist, *The Marginal Man: A Study of Personality and Cultural Conflict* (New York: Russell & Russell, 1937), 8.

2. Charles Marden and Gladys Meyer, *Minorities in American Society* (New York: Van Nostrand Reinhold, 1968), 44–45.

3. Stonequist, *The Marginal Man*, 221.

4. H. F. Dickie-Clark, *The Marginal Situation: A Sociological Study of a Colored Group* (London: Routledge & Kegan Paul, 1966), 24, 31.

5. Peter C. Phan, "Betwixt and Between: Doing Theology with Memory and Imagination," in *Journeys at the Margin: Toward an Autobiographical Theology in American-Asian Perspectives*, ed. Peter Phan and Jung Young Lee (Collegeville, Minn: Liturgical, 1999), 113.

6. See, for example, Uriah Yong-Hwan Kim, "The Realpolitik of Liminality in Josiah's Kingdom and Asian America," Mary F. Foskett and Jeffrey Kuan, eds., *Ways of Being, Ways of Reading: Asian American Biblical Hermenuetics* (St. Louis: Chalice, 2006), 84–98; Sze-kar Wan, "Betwixt and Between: Toward a Hermeneutics of Hyphenation," ibid., 137–51; Jung Young Lee, "A Life In-Between: A Korean-American Journey," in Phan and Lee, *Journeys at the Margin*, 23–39.

7. bell hooks, *Yearning: Race, Gender and Cultural Politics* (Boston: South End, 1990), 153.

8. Victor W. Turner, *Ritual Process: Structure and Anti-Structure* (Ithaca: Cornell University Press, 1969), 94ff.

9. Ibid., 139.

10. Won Moo Hurh, "Comparative Study of Korean Immigrants in the U.S.: A Typological Study," in Byong-suh Kim, et al., eds., *Koreans in America*

(Memphis: Association of Korean Christian Scholars in North America, 1997), 95.

11. Won Moo Hurh and Kwang Chung Kim, *Korean Immigrants in America: A Structural Analysis of Ethnic Confinement and Adhesive Adaptation* (Rutherford, N.J.: Fairleigh Dickinson University Press, 1984), 86.

12. Ibid., 89.

13. Turner, *Ritual Process*, 94–130.

14. Ibid., 95.

15. Victor W. Turner, *From Ritual to Theatre: The Seriousness of Human Play* (New York: Performance Art Journal Publications, 1982), 28.

16. Turner, *Ritual Process*, vii.

17. Ibid., 95.

18. William Bridges, *Transitions: Making Sense of Life's Changes* (Reading, Mass.: Andover-Wesley, 1980), 199.

19. Turner, *Ritual Process*, 96.

20. Turner, *Drama, Fields, and Metaphors: Symbolic Action in Human Society* (Ithaca: Cornell University Press, 1974), 269.

21. Ibid., 68

22. Turner, *Ritual Process*, 128.

23. Ibid., 128.

24. Ibid., 129.

25. Turner, *Drama, Fields, and Metaphors*, 243.

26. Bobby C. Alexander, *Victor Turner Revisited: Ritual as Social Change* (Atlanta: Scholars), 41.

27. Turner, *From Ritual to Theatre*, 27

28. Ibid., 47

29. Turner, *Drama, Fields, and Metaphors*, 274.

30. Alexander, *Turner Revisited*, 23.

31. Turner, *Ritual Process*, vii.

32. Ibid.

33. Paul Shepard, "Study Says Race Determines Type of Justice Americans Receive," *Asian Week* 21, no. 37 (May 17, 2000): 17.

34. Gilbert C. Gee, Michael S, Spencer, Juan Chen, and David Takeuchi, "A Nationwide Study of Discrimination and Chronic Health Conditions Among Asian Americans," *American Journal of Public Health* 97, no. 7 (July 2007): 3–4.

35. Kwang Chung Kim and Won Moo Hurh, "The 'Success' Image of Asian Americans: Its Validity and Its Practical and Theoretical Implications," *Ethnic and Racial Studies* 22 (October 1989): 531.

36. Wesley Woo, "Asians in America: Challenges to the Presbyterian Church (U.S.A.)," an unpublished paper, May 1987, 13.

37. Gary Y. Okihiro, *Margins and Mainstreams: Asians in American History and Culture* (Seattle: University of Washington Press, 1994), 62.

38. Elaine H. Kim, "Creating a Third Space," *San Francisco Bay Guardian*, March 10, 1993.

39. Hurh and Kim, *Korean Immigrants in America*, 146–49.

40. Joe R. Feagin, *Racial and Ethnic Relations* (Englewood, N.J.: Prentice-Hall, 1989), 15.

41. Joe Feagin, "The Continuing Significance of Race: Anti-Black Discrimination in Public Places," *American Sociological Review* 56 (February 1991): 115.

42. Derald Wing Sue, et al., "Racial Microaggressions and the Asian American Experience," *Cultural Diversity & Ethnic Minority Psychology* 13, no. 1 (January 2007): 72–81.

43. Ibid., 72.

44. Ibid.

45. Ibid., 73.

46. Ibid., 75–77

47. Gloria Yamato, "Something About the Subject Makes It Hard to Name," in Margaret Anderson and Patricia Collins, eds., *Race, Class and Gender* (Belmont, Cal.: Wadsworth, 2001), 91–92.

48. Elaine H. Kim, "Poised on the In-between: A Korean American's Reflections on Theresa Hak Kyung Cha's Dictee," in Elaine H. Kim and Norma Alarcon, eds., *Writing Self/Writing Nation* (Berkeley: Third Woman, 1994), 21.

49. Penelope Washburn, *Becoming Woman: The Quest for Wholeness in Female Experience* (New York: Harper & Row, 1977), 22, 23, 26.

50. Carol Christ, *Diving Deep and Surfacing: Women Writers on Spiritual Quest* (Boston: Beacon, 1980), 13.

51. Rita Nakashima Brock, "Interstitial Integrity," in Roger A. Badham, ed., *Introduction to Christian Theology: Contemporary North American Perspectives* (Louisville: Westminster John Knox, 1998), 190–91.

52. Ibid., 187.

53. Inn Sook Lee, *Passage to the Real Self: The Development of Self-Integration for Asian American Women* (Lanham, Md.: University Press of America, 2009), 105–33.

54. Ibid., 106, 113, 123.

55. Esther Ngan-Ling Chow, "The Feminist Movement: Where Are All the Asian American Women?" in Asian Women United of California, eds., *Making Waves: An Anthology of Writings by and about Asian American Women* (Boston: Beacon, 1989), 367–68.

56. Kwang Chung Kim and Won Moo Hurh, "The Wives of Korean Small Businessmen in the U.S.: Business Involvement and Family Roles," in Inn Sook Lee, ed., *Korean American Women: Toward Self-Realization* (Mansfield, Oh.: The Association of Korean Christian Scholars in North America, 1989), 23.

57. Ibid.

58. Ai Ra Kim, *Women Struggling for a New Life* (Albany: State University of New York Press, 1996), 72-73.

59. Hwain Chang Lee, *Confucius, Christ and Co-Partnership: Competing Liturgies for the Soul of Korean American Women* (Lanham, Md.: University Press of America, 1994), 12.

60. Ai Ra Kim, *Women Struggling for a New Life*, 71.

61. Peter Cha and Grace May, "Gender Relations in Healthy Households," in Peter Chan, S. Steve Kang, and Helen Lee, eds., *Growing Healthy Asian American Churches* (Downer's Grove, Ill.: InterVarsity Press, 2006), 165.

62. Hurh and Kim, *Korean Immigrants in America*, 73–86.

63. Won Moo Hurh, "Comparative Study of Korean Immigrants in the U.S.," 95.

64. Ronald Takaki, *Strangers from a Different Shore: A History of Asian Americans* (Englewood Cliffs, N.J.: Prentice-Hall, 1988), 75. See also Harry H. L. Kitano and Roger Daniels, *Asian Americans: Emerging Minorities* (Englewood Cliffs, N.J.: Prentice-Hall, 1988), 2.

CHAPTER TWO

1. Robert L. Cohn, "Liminality in the Wilderness," in Robert L. Cohn, *The Shape of Sacred Space: Four Biblical Studies,* AAR Studies in Religion 23 (Chico, Calif.: Scholars, 1981), 22–23.

2. Ernst Lohmeyer, *Galiläa und Jerusalem* (Göttingen: Vandenhoeck & Ruprecht, 1936); R. H. Lightfoot, *Locality and Doctrine in the Gospels* (London: Hodder & Stoughton, 1938).

3. See, for example, Elizabeth Struthers Malbon, "Galilee and Jerusalem: History and Literature in Marcan Interpretation," *Catholic Biblical Quarterly* 44 (1982): 242–55; Günter Stemberger, "Galilee—Land of Salvation?" in W. D. Davies, *The Gospel and the Land* (Berkeley: University of California Press, 1974), 409–38.

4. See, for example, Richard A. Horsley, *Sociology and the Jesus Movement* (New York: Continuum, 1994). Mexican American theologian Virgilio Elizondo pioneered the use of biblical studies on Galilee in a contextual theology. He interprets the meaning of the *mestizaje* of his people in light of God's choice of Galileans for God's special purposes. Elizondo believes that "what the world rejects, God chooses as his very own." Elizondo, however, does not theorize about the reasons for God's choice of Galileans. Virgilio Elizondo, *Galilean Journey: The Mexican-American Promise* (Maryknoll, N.Y.: Orbis, 1983), 53.

5. Sean Freyne, *Galilee, Jesus, and the Gospels: Literary Approaches and Historical Investigations* (Philadelphia: Fortress Press, 1988), 78.

6. Horsley, *Sociology and the Jesus Movement*, 105, 111, 113, 114.

7. Freyne, *Galilee, Jesus, and the Gospels*, 54.

8. L. E. Elliott-Binns, *Galilean Christianity* (London: SCM, 1956), 27; Anne Hennessy, *The Galilee of Jesus* (Rome: Editrice Pontificia Università Gregoriana, 1994), 14–18.

9. In describing the liminality and marginalization of Galilee and Galileans, I am much dependent on the information provided by Freyne, *Galilee, Jesus, and the Gospels*, and Hennessy, *The Galilee of Jesus*, in addition to Horsley's *Galilee: History, Politics, and People* (New York: Continuum, 1995).

10. Horsley, *Galilee: History, Politics, and People*, 29, 47.

11. Ibid., 25.

12. Ibid., 71.

13. Ibid., 26–27, 243.

14. Ibid., 147.

15. Ibid., 24.

16. Ibid., 219.

17. William R. Herzog II, *Jesus, Justice and the Reign of God: A Ministry of Liberation* (Louisville: Westminster John Knox, 2000), 122–23.

18. James C. Scott, *Weapons of the Weak: Of the Everyday Forms of Peasant Resistance* (New Haven: Yale University Press, 1985), 1–47.

CHAPTER THREE

1. Jonathan Edwards, "Miscellanies," No. 104, in *The "Miscellanies," a–500*, ed. Thomas A. Schafer, vol. 13 of *The Works of Jonathan Edwards* (New Haven: Yale University Press, 1994), 272.

2. Jonathan Edwards, "Concerning the End for Which God Created the World," in *Ethical Writings*, ed. Paul Ramsey, vol. 8 in *The Works of Jonathan Edwards* (New Haven: Yale University Press, 1989), 433.

3. Ibid., 443, 534. For a fuller discussion of this matter, see Sang Hyun Lee, *The Philosophical Theology of Jonathan Edwards* (Princeton: Princeton University Press, 1988), esp. 170–210.

4. Jonathan Edwards, "Discourse on the Trinity," in *Writings on the Trinity, Grace, and Faith*, ed. Sang Hyun Lee, vol. 21 of *The Works of Jonathan Edwards* (New Haven: Yale University Press, 2003), 114.

5. Hans Urs von Balthasar, *Mysterium and Paschale: The Mystery of Easter*, viii, quoted in Margaret M. Turek, *Towards a Theology of the Father: Hans Urs von Balthasar's Theodramatic Approach* (New York: Peter Lang, 2001), 106.

6. Ibid.

7. Hans Urs von Balthasar, *The Action*, trans. Graham Harrison, vol. 4 of *Theo-Drama: Theological Dramatic Theory* (San Francisco: Ignatius, 1994), 323–24.

8. Hans Urs von Balthasar, *The Last Act*, trans. Graham Harrison, vol. 5 of *Theo-Drama: Theological Dramatic Theory* (San Francisco: Ignatius, 1994), 94.

9. Von Balthasar, *The Action*, 4:323.

10. Turek, *Towards a Theology of the Father*, 125.

11. Ibid., 126.

12. Hans Urs von Balthasar, *Dramatis Personae: Man in God*, vol. 2 of *Theo-Drama: Theological Dramatic Theory* (San Francisco: Ignatius, 1990), 257 (emphasis mine).

13. Von Balthasar, *The Action*, 4:324.

14. Hans Urs von Balthasar, *Word and Redemption: Essays in Theology 2*, trans. A. V. Littledale (New York: Herder & Herder, 1965), 33–34, quoted in Turek, *Towards a Theology of the Father*, 107.

15. Gregory of Nazianzus, Epistle 101, in *Christology of the Later Fathers*, ed. Edward R. Hardy, Library of Christian Classics, vol. 3 (Philadelphia: Westminster, 1954), 218.

CHAPTER FOUR

1. Walter Kasper, *Jesus the Christ* (Mahwah, N.J.: Paulist, 1979), 79.

2. John P. Meier, *The Roots of the Problem and the Person*, vol. 1 of *A Marginal Jew: Rethinking the Historical Jesus* (New York: Doubleday, 1991), 407.

3. Halvor Moxnes, *Putting Jesus in His Place: A Radical Vision of Household and Kingdom* (Louisville: Westminster John Knox, 2003), 46–49.

4. Ibid., 55, 68, 70.

5. Ibid., 53.

6. Moxnes explores other possible reasons why the women followers of Jesus were not asked to leave their homes suddenly as men were (ibid., 98–101).

7. Ross Kraemer, *Her Share of Blessings: Women's Religions among Pagans, Jews, and Christians in the Greco-Roman World* (New York: Oxford University Press, 1992), 133.

8. Moxnes, *Putting Jesus in His Place*, 100.

9. Victor W. Turner, *Ritual Process*, 128.

10. John P. Meier, *Companions and Competitors*, vol. 3 of *A Marginal Jew: Rethinking the Historical Jesus* (New York: Doubleday, 2001), 5.

11. Turner, *Ritual Process*, 132,137, 140. .

12. Ibid., 129.

13. Moxnes, *Putting Jesus in His Place*, 129.

14. Ibid., 122.

15. Bruce J. Malina and Richard L. Rohrbaugh, *Social-Science Commentary on the Synoptic Gospels* (Minneapolis: Fortress Press, 2003), 363, quoted in William R. Herzog II, *Jesus, Justice and the Reign of God*, 184.

16. Ibid., 213.

17. Ibid., 214.

18. Ibid.

19. Cf. Jürgen Moltmann, *The Crucified God: The Cross of Christ as the Foundation and Criticism of Christian Theology*, trans. R. A. Wilson and John Bowden (Minneapolis: Fortress Press, 1993 [1974]), 242-43.

20. Ibid., 245.

21. Wonhee Anne Joh, *Heart of the Cross: A Postcolonial Christology* (Louisville: Westminster John Knox, 2006), 76–77.

22. Jürgen Moltmann, *The Way of Jesus Christ*, trans. Margaret Kohl (Minneapolis: Fortress Press, 1993 [1990]), 186.

23. Kasper, *Jesus the Christ*, 156.

24. Ibid., 145.

CHAPTER FIVE

1. Daniel L. Migliore, *Faith Seeking Understanding: An Introduction to Christian Theology*, 2d ed. (Grand Rapids: Eerdmans, 2004), 183.

2. Ibid., 184.

3. Ibid. See also Bruce McCormack, *For Us and Our Salvation: Incarnation and Atonement in the Reformed Tradition*, Studies in Reformed Theology and History 1 (Spring 1993).

4. Migliore, *Faith Seeking Understanding*, 185. See also Philip Quinn, "Abelard on Atonement: 'Nothing Unintelligible, Arbitrary, Illogical, or Immoral about It," In *Reasoned Faith*, ed. Eleanore Stump (Ithaca: Cornell University Press, 1993), 296.

5. Wonhee Anne Joh, *Heart of the Cross: A Postcolonial Christology* (Louisville: Westminster John Knox, 2006), 106.

6. Daniel Day Williams, *The Spirit and Forms of Love* (New York: Harper & Row, 1968), 183.

7. Andrew Sung Park, *From Hurt to Healing: A Theology of the Wounded* (Nashville: Abingdon, 2004), 11.

8. Wendy Farley, *Tragic Vision and Divine Compassion: A Contemporary Theodicy* (Louisville: Westminster John Knox, 1990), 7.

9. Ibid., 8.

10. Ibid., 117.

11. Rita Nakashima Brock, *Journeys by Heart: A Christology of Erotic Power* (New York: Crossroad, 1996), 26, 67.

12. Wonhee Anne Joh, "Violence and Asian American Experience: From Abjection to Jeung," in Rita Nakashima Brock, Jung Ha Kim, Kwok Pui-lan, and Seung-Ai Yang, eds., *Off the Menu: Asian and Asian North American Women's Religion and Theology* (Louisville: Westminster John Knox, 2007), 149.

13. Ibid., 146, 156.

14. Joh, *Heart of the Cross*, 122.

15. Ibid., 121.

16. Park, *From Hurt to Healing*, 132; Brock, *Journeys by Heart*, 52; Joh, "Violence and Asian American Experience," 151.

17. Jonathan Edwards, "Faith," in *Writings on the Trinity, Grace, and Faith*, ed. Sang Hyun Lee, vol. 21 of *The Works of Jonathan Edwards* (New Haven: Yale University Press, 2003), 436.

18. Ibid.

19. Søren Kierkegaard, *Philosophical Fragments*, ed. and trans. Howard Hong and Edna Hong (Princeton: Princeton University Press, 1985), 55–110.

20. Park, *From Hurt to Healing*, 4–7, 16, 105–6.

21. Harold Wells, "Theology of Reconciliation: Biblical Perspectives on Forgiveness and Grace," in Gregory Baum and Harold Wells, eds., *The Reconciliation of Peoples: Challenge to the Churches* (Maryknoll, N.Y.: Orbis, 1997), 12.

22. John Calvin, *Institutes of the Christian Religion*, ed. John T. McNeill (Philadelphia: Westminster, 1960), III.Iii.1-2, 592–94.

23. Ibid., III.iii.8-9, 600–601.

24. Paul Tillich, *Systematic Theology, Vol. 2: Existence and the Christ* (Chicago: University of Chicago Press, 1957), 40.

25. On Korean American and African American relations, see, for example, Kwang Chung Kim, ed., *Koreans in the Hood: Conflict with African Americans* (Baltimore: Johns Hopkins University Press, 1999).

26. Andrew Sung Park, *Racial Conflict and Healing: An Asian-American Theological Perspective* (Maryknoll, N.Y.: Orbis, 1996), 41–47.

27. Kwang Chung Kim and Won Moo Hurh, "The Wives of Korean Small Businessmen in the U.S.: Business Involvement and Family Roles," in Inn Sook Lee, ed., *Korean-American Women* (Mansfield, Ohio: Association of Korean Christian Scholars in North America, 1985), 19–24.

28. Young I. Song and Ailee Moon, "The Domestic Violence against Women in Korean Immigrant Families: Cultural, Psychological and Socioeconomic Perspectives," in Young I. Song and Ailee Moon, eds., *Korean American Women: From Tradition to Modern Feminism* (Westport, Conn.: Praeger, 1998), 162–63.

29. Fumitaka Matsuoka, *Out of Silence: Emerging Themes in Asian American Churches* (Cleveland: United Church Press, 1995), 96.

CHAPTER SIX

1. Stuart Hall, "Cultural Identity and Diaspora," in Jonathan Rutherford, ed., *Identity: Community, Culture, Difference* (London: Lawrence and Wishart, 1990), 226, 225.

2. Calvin O. Schrag, *The Self after Postmodernity* (New Haven: Yale University Press, 1997), 21, 60.

3. Ibid., 58.

4. Bill Ashcroft, Gareth Griffiths and Helen Tiffin, *Post-Colonial Studies: The Key Concepts* (London: Routledge, 1998), 120.

5. Homi Bhabha, "Culture's In-Between," in Stuart Hall and Paul de Gay, eds., *Questions of Cultural Identity* (London: Sage, 1996), 54.

6. Homi Bhabha, *The Location of Culture* (London: Routledge, 1994), 56.

7. Bhabha, "Culture's In-Between," 58.

8. Ibid., 54.

9. Bhabha, *The Location of Culture*, 56.

10. Gary Y. Okihiro, *Margins and Mainstreams: Asians in American History and Culture* (Seattle: University of Washington Press, 1994), 171, 174.

11. Ibid., 175.

12. Gale A. Yee makes a similar point about this photograph. See her essay "'She Stood in Tears amid the Alien Corn': Ruth, the Perpetual Foreigner and Model Minority," in Rita Nakashima Brock, Jung Ha Kim, Kwok Pui-Lan, Sung Ai Yang, eds., *Off the Menu: Asian and Asian North American Women's Religion and Theology* (Louisville: Westminster John Knox, 2007), 60 n.62.

13. Fumitaka Matsuoka, *Out of Silence: Emerging Themes in Asian American Churches* (Cleveland: United Church Press, 1995), 62.

14. Rita Nakashima Brock, "Interstitial Integrity: Reflections toward an Asian American Woman's Theology," in Roger A. Badham, ed., *Introduction to Christian Theology: Contemporary North American Perspectives* (Louisville: Westminster John Knox, 1988), 191.

15. Rita Nakashima Brock, "Cooking Without Recipes: Interstitial Integrity," in Rita Nakashima Brock, et al., eds., *Off the Menu*, 140.

16. Brock, "Interstitial Integrity," in Badham, ed., *Introduction to Christian Theology*, 191.

17. Ibid., 190.

18. Ibid.

19. Stephen Crites, "The Narrative Quality of Experience," *Journal of American Academy of Religion* 39, no. 3 (September, 1971): 302, 303.

20. Fred B. Craddock, "The Letter to the Hebrews," in *Hebrews, James, 1 & 2 Peter, 1, 2, & 3 John, Jude, Revelation*, vol. 12 of *The New Interpreter's Bible* (Nashville: Abingdon, 1998), 137.

CHAPTER SEVEN

1. Victor Turner, *The Ritual Process: Structure and Anti-Structure* (Ithaca: Cornell University Press, 1977), 132; Victor Turner and Edith Turner, *Image and Pilgrimage in Christian Culture: Anthropological Perspectives* (New York: Columbia University Press, 1978), 252.

2. Turner, *The Ritual Process*, 137.

3. Ibid., 139.

4. Turner and Turner, *Image and Pilgrimage*, 252.

5. Turner, *The Ritual Process*, 129.

6. Ibid., 139.

7. Ibid.

8. Ibid., 132.

9. Victor Turner, *Dramas, Fields, and Metaphors: Symbolic Action in Human Society* (Ithaca: Cornell University Press, 1996), 250.

10. Avery Dulles, S.J., *Models of the Church* (Garden City, N.Y.: Doubleday, 1974), 45–46.

11. Won Moo Hurh and Kwang Chung Kim, *Korean Immigrants in America: A Structural Analysis of Ethnic Confinement and Adhesive Adaptation* (Rutherford, N.J.: Fairleigh Dickinson University Press, 1984), 129–37.

12. Robert L. Moore, "Ministry, Sacred Space, and Theological Education: The Legacy of Victor Turner," *The Chicago Theological Seminary Register* 75, no. 3 (Fall, 1985): 6.

13. Ibid., 5.

14. John Calvin, *Institutes of the Christian Religion*, ed. John T. McNeill (Philadelphia: Westminster, 1960), IV.1.9, 1023.

15. See William R. Herzog II, *Jesus, Justice, and the Reign of God: A Ministry of Liberation* (Louisville: Westminster John Knox, 2000), 111ff.

16. Ibid., 213–14.

17. Peter Cha, "Journey of Reconciliation and Justice," unpublished paper, 6.

18. Peter Cha, "A Church for the Misfit and Marginalized: An Interview with David Gibbons," unpublished paper, 1-3.

19. On this point, I found helpful the following: Rosita Dean Mathews, "Using Power from the Periphery: An Alternative Theological Model for Survival in Systems," in Emilie M. Townes, ed., *A Troubling in My Soul: Womanist Perspectives on Evil and Suffering* (Maryknoll, N.Y.: Orbis, 1993), 92–107.

20. "A Church for the Misfit and Marginalized," 9.

21. Ibid., 10.

22. For the full account of the Oak Park story, see Russell Jeung, "Faith-Based, Multiethnic Tenant Organizing," in Pierrette Hondagneu-Sotelo, ed., *Religion and Social Justice for Immigrants* (New Brunswick, N.J.: Rutgers University Press, 2007), 59–73.

23. See, for example, Ai Ra Kim, *Women Struggling for a New Life: The Role of Religion in the Cultural Passage from Korea to America* (Albany: State University of New York Press, 1996), 72–73; Inn Sook Lee, *Passage to the Real Self: The Development of Self-Integration for Asian American Women* (Lanham, Md.: University Press of America, 2009), 41.

24. Peter Cha, S. Steve Kang, and Helen Lee, *Growing Healthy Asian American Churches: Ministry Insights from Groundbreaking Congregations* (Downers Grove, Ill.: IVP, 2006), 42.

25. Jung Ha Kim, *Bridge-Makers and Cross-Bearers: Korean-American Women and the Church* (Atlanta: Scholars, 1997), 108.

26. See James C. Scott, *Domination and the Arts of Resistance: Hidden Transcripts* (New Haven: Yale University Press, 1990).

27. Elaine H. Kim, "Poised on the In-Between: A Korean-American's Reflections on Teresa Hak Kyung Cha's Dictee," in Elaine H. Kim and Norma Alarcon, eds., *Writing Self/Writing Nation* (Berkeley: Third Woman, 1994); Penelope Washbourn, *Becoming Woman: A Quest for Wholeness in Female Experience* (New York: Harper & Row, 1977); Carol Christ, *Diving Deep and Surfacing: Women Writers on Spiritual Quest* (Boston: Beacon, 1980); Inn Sook Lee, *Passage to the Real Self*, 57ff.

28. Elisabeth Schüssler Fiorenza, *In Memory of Her: A Feminist Theological Reconstruction of Christian Origins* (New York: Crossroad, 1986), 320.

29. Ibid., 332.

30. Ibid., 323.

31. From a phone conversation with Pastor Kim, July, 2009.

32. From a conversation with several Caucasian members of the church, April, 2009.

33. Jacob Milgrom, "Holy, Holiness, OT," in *The New Interpreter's Dictionary of the Bible*, vol. 2 (Nashville: Abingdon, 2007), 850.

34. Alister E. McGrath, *Christian Theology: An Introduction* (Oxford: Blackwell, 1997), 488.

35. See John H. Elliott, *A Home for the Homeless: A Sociological Exegesis of 1 Peter—Its Situation and Strategy* (Philadelphia: Fortress Press, 1981), 122, 127.

36. Edward Farley, *Ecclesial Man: A Social Phenomenology of Faith and Reality* (Philadelphia: Fortress Press, 1975), 158; Mark Kline Taylor, *Remembering Esperanza: A Cultural-Political Theology for North American Praxis* (Maryknoll, N.Y.: Orbis, 1990), 206.

37. Ibid., 205.

38. Fumitaka Matsuoka, *Out of Silence: Emerging Themes in Asian American Churches* (Cleveland: United Church Press, 1995), 96.

CHAPTER EIGHT

1. See Lisa Lowe, *Immigrant Acts: On Asian American Cultural Politics* (Durham: Duke University Press, 1996), 60ff.

2. H. Richard Niebuhr, *The Meaning of Revelation* (New York: Macmillan, 1962), 116.

3. Mark Kline Taylor, *Remembering Esperanza: A Cultural-Political Theology for North American Praxis* (Maryknoll, N.Y.: Orbis, 1990), 199.

4. Anselm Kyungsuk Min, *Solidarity of Others in a Divided World: A Postmodern Theology after Postmodernism* (New York: T&T Clark, 2004), 139.

5. Ibid., 141.

6. Ibid., 85, 124, 128.

7. Ibid., 230, 144.

8. John B. Cobb, *Resistance: The New Role of Progressive Christians* (Louisville: Westminster John Knox, 2008).

9. Virgilio Elizondo, *Galilean Journey: The Mexican-American Promise* (Maryknoll, N.Y.: Orbis, 1997), 120.

10. Leander E. Keck, "Matthew," in *New Testament Articles, Matthew, Mark*, vol. 8 of *The New Interpreter's Bible* (Nashville: Abingdon, 1995), 176.

11. Leroy S. Rouner, *In Pursuit of Happiness* (Notre Dame, Ind.: University of Notre Dame Press, 1995).

12. See, for example, *The Miscellanies a-500*, ed. Thomas A. Schafer, vol. 13 of *The Works of Jonathan Edwards* (New Haven: Yale University Press, 1994), nos. 87, 106.

13. Albert Camus, *Lyrical and Critical Essays* (New York: Vintage, 1970), 101–2; idem, *The Plague* (New York: Knopf, 1968), 232.

14. Miroslav Volf, *Exclusion and Embrace: A Theological Exploration of Identity, Otherness, and Reconciliation* (Nashville: Abingdon, 1996), 134, 135–36.

15. See Joanne Doi, "Tule Lake Pilgrimage: Dissonant Memories, Sacred Journey," in Jane Iwamura and Paul Spickard, eds., *Revealing the Sacred in Asian and Pacific America* (New York: Routledge, 2003), 273–89.

CHAPTER NINE

1. Fumitaka Matsuoka, *The Color of Faith: Building Community in a Multiracial Society* (Cleveland: United Church Press, 1998), 2.

2. James H. Cone, *God of the Oppressed* (New York: Seabury, 1975), 238, 243.

3. Miroslav Volf, *Exclusion and Embrace: A Theological Exploration of Identity, Otherness, and Reconciliation* (Nashville: Abingdon, 1996), 110.

4. John W. de Gruchy, *Reconciliation: Restoring Justice* (Minneapolis: Fortress Press, 2002), 26.

5. Volf, *Exclusion and Embrace*, 201.

6. Ibid., 213–14, 218, 224.

7. John Calvin, *Institutes of the Christian Religion*, ed. John T. McNeill, The Library of Christian Classics XX (Philadelphia: Westminster, 1960), III. Xvi. 1

8. Volf, *Exclusion and Embrace*, 129.

9. Ibid., 141-42.

10. Ibid., 142

11. Ibid., 143.

12. Ibid., 165

13. A white male seminary intern working at the church.

14. Jin S. Kim, "A Story of the Church of All Nations," *PC (USA)/ Multicultural Congregational Support*, May 5, 2009; Heather Roote Faller, "Spirit Moves in Multicultural Ways: Becoming a Church of All Nations," *inSpire* (Fall 2008/ Winter/Spring, 2009): 33.

15. Conversation with Jin S. Kim, May 2009

16. Joanne Doi, "Tule Lake Pilgrimage: Dissonant Memories, Sacred Journey," in *Revealing the Sacred in Asian and Pacific America*, ed. Jane Naomi Iwamura and Paul Spickard (New York: Routledge, 2003), quoting Victor Turner, "Death and the Dead in the Pilgrimage Process," in *Religious Encounters with Death*, ed. Frank E. Reynolds and Earl H. Waugh (University Park: Pennsylvania State University Press, 1977), 38-39.

CHAPTER TEN

1. See Paul Ramsey, "Appendix III. Heaven Is a Progressive State," in *Ethical Writings*, ed. Paul Ramsey, vol. 8 of *The Works of Jonathan Edwards* (New Haven: Yale University Press, 1989), 706–38.

2. Jonathan Edwards, "The End for Which God Created the World," in ibid., 8:443, 536.

3. Ibid., 8:433.

4. Ramsey, "Appendix III. Heaven Is a Progressive State," in ibid., 8:723.

5. Ibid., 8:720–24.

6. Daniel L. Migliore, *Faith Seeking Understanding: An Introduction to Christian Theology*, 2d ed. (Grand Rapids: Eerdmans, 2004), 339.

7. Benjamin Reist, *Theology in Red, White, and Black* (Philadelphia: Westminster, 1975), 183.

8. Albert Camus, *The Plague* (New York: Vintage International, 1991), 224.

9. Jürgen Moltmann, *The Theology of Hope*, trans. James W. Leitch (New York: Harper & Row, 1967), 21.

INDEX

Abelard, Peter, 91
Alexander, Bobby, 10
ancestor worship, 116–17
Anselm, 90–91
Aquinas, Thomas, 55
Asian American Church: as liminal
    space and *communitas*, 123–26
    prophetic function of 132–35
    as refuge, 127–28
    and women, 138–41
assimilation: cultural and struc-
    tural, 29
    of non-white immigrants, 30
atonement: and healing, 94–96
    theories of, 89–91
Augustine of Hippo, 132

Barth, Karl, 91
beatific vision, 176
Bhabha, Homi, 110–12
Bridges, William, 8
Brock, Nakashima Rita, 24, 95–96,
    118–19

Brueggemann, Walter, 37

Calvin, John, 104, 131, 164
Camus, Albert, 158, 178
Capernaum, 39, 45–46, 68
Carson, Timothy L., 129
Cha, Peter, 28, 39, 134, 138
Cha, Teresa Hak Kyung, 22, 139
Chow, Esther Ngan-Ling, 25
Christ, Carol, 23–29, 139
Church of All Nations (Minneapo-
    lis), 138, 143, 167, 169
Cobb, Jr., John B., 156
Cohn, Robert L., 37
communitas, 8–9
    church as, 124–38
    as Holy Spirit 55, 59
    ideological, 124
    normative, 124
    and reconciliation, 166–71
    "spontaneous or existential," 124
Cone, James, 161–64
Constantinople, Council of, 141

197

Crites, Stephen, 119–20

de Gruchy, John, 162
Dickie-Clark, H. F., 3
Doi, Joanne, 170–71
Dulles, Avery, 125–26

Edwards, Jonathan, 52–55, 98, 163, 173–74
Elliott-Binns, L. E., 44
Executive Order 9066, 169

family of God, 74–76, 123, 147
Farley, Edward, 145
Farley, Wendy, 94
Feagan, Joe, 17–18
Freyne, Sean, 39–40, 43

Galilee: as liminal place, 43–47
  as marginalized place, 47–49
  as primary place of Jesus' ministry, 38–43
Gibbons, David, 134, 136–37, 147
God: dispositional essence of, 52
  as distinguished from the world, 53
  fullness of, 52
  immutability and simplicity of, 55
  internal actuality of, 53
  and liminal and marginalized people, 35–37
  liminality of, 54–59
  repetition *ad extra* of internal actuality of, 53
Gregory of Nazianzus, 61

Hall, Stuart, 109
han, 94
Hennessy, Anne, 44
Herzog, William, 78
Holy Spirit: as *communitas* between the Father and the Son, 55, 61, 71
hooks, bell, 5
Horsley, Richard A. 38, 42–43, 44–45
Hurh, Won Moo, 14, 26, 30
hybridity, 110–12

identity: of Asian Americans, 112–17
  and faith,117–19
  and narrative, 119–22
immanent Trinity, 59
interstitial integrity, 118–19
interstitiality, 24–25
"isolated discrimination," 16
issei, 170

Jesus Christ: and *communitas* with others, 70–76
  death of, 79–83
  exaltation of, 86–87
  infinite liminality of, 80–83, 97–99
  and leaving home, 64–66
  resistance against the oppressors by, 76–79
  resurrection of, 83–86
  women in the ministry of, 67, 83, 139–41
jeung, 92, 95
Jeung, Russell, 137

Joh, Wonhee Anne, 81, 92, 95–96

Kasper, Walter, 85, 87
Kierkegaard, Søren, 100
Kim, Ai Ra, 27
Kim, Elaine H., 15, 22
Kim, Jin S., 143, 167, 169
Kim, Jung Ha, 138
Kim, Kwang Chung, 14, 26
Korean immigrant church, 26–28, 127–28, 133, 142
Kraemer, Ross, 67

Lee, Inn Sook, 25, 137
Lightfoot, R. H., 38
liminality, 4–11
    of Asian American women, 22–25
    of Asian Americans, 1–5
    in condition of marginalization, 31–33
    creative potentials of, 7–11
    as distinguished from marginality, 5
    of Galilee and Galileans, 43–47
    and identity, 117–18
    and the incarnation, 59–61
    of Jesus on the cross, 80–83
    and reconciliation, 164–71
    subjective and objective, 64
Lohmeyer, Ernst, 38
Lord's Supper: and liminality, 129–30
Lowe, Lisa, 149

Malina, Bruce, 77

marginality, 2–5
    and liminality, 5
marginalization, 4–5
    of Asian American women, 22–28
    of Asian Americans, 11–21
    of Galileans, 47–49
Mary and Martha in Bethany, 67, 69, 82
Mary Magdalene, 67, 72, 77, 83, 139, 140
Matsuoka, Fumitaka, 108, 118, 145–46, 161
May, Grace, 28, 138
McGrath, Alister, 144
Meier, John P., 72
mental health of Asian Americans, 13
Migliore, Daniel, 90
Min, Anselm Kyungsuk, 153–54
model minority: critique of, 14
Moltmann, Jürgen, 81, 84
Moore, Robert L, 129
Moxnes, Halvor, 65–67, 75

New Song Community Church (Los Angeles), 147
Nicaea, Council of, 141
Niebuhr, H. Richard, 150
nisei, 170

Oak Park Ministries, 137
Okihiro, Gary Y., 15, 114
original kenosis, 56

Park, Andrew Sung, 94, 96, 102–3, 107

Park, Robert E., 2
Phan, Peter C., 3–4

racial microaggression, 18–20
Reist, Benjamin, 177
Rohr, Richard, 135
Rohrbaugh, Richard, 77

Schrag, Paul, 110, 119
Schüssler Fiorenza, Elisabeth, 141
Scott, James C., 49, 139
Stonequist, Everett, 2
Susanna, 77
Syro-Phoencian woman, 140

Takaki, Ronald, 30
Taylor, Mark Lewis, 145, 152
Third Space, 111–12

Tillich, Paul, 106
Turek, Margaret, 57
Turner, Victor, 5–6, 9–10, 58, 65, 70, 74, 124–27, 153

Volf, Miroslav, 158–59; 162–66
von Balthasar, Hans Urs, 55–59
von Gennep, Arnold, 5

Washburn, Penelope, 23
Wells, Harold, 104
Williams, Daniel Day, 92
Woo, Wesley, 15
worship and liminality, 128–29

Yamato, Gloria, 20–21

Zacchaeus, 69–71,82